BEST OF
CHEF
LOU
& A LITTLE MORE

Chef Lou Rice is currently the Divisions Chair of Culinary Arts and Hospitality for Ozarks Technical Community College in Springfield, Missouri, which is located in the foothills of the Ozarks. He is a certified Chef de Cuisine by the American Culinary Federation as well as a certified hospitality educator by the American Hotel and Lodging Association. He has degrees in psychology, culinary arts and a master's degree in consumer science. Chef Lou has cooked and taught at country clubs, privately owned operations, several colleges, and, of course, his restaurant the stories from which could easily make its own book.

JEC PUBLISHING COMPANY
2049 E. Cherry St., Suite 100
Springfield, Missouri 65802
(800) 313-5121

Copyright © 2007 by Lou Rice

Library of Congress Control Number: 2007936111

ISBN: 978-0-9778057-6-1

Editorial Coordinator: Stacy Rice

Publication Production: JE Cornwell

Cover Design and Graphics Layout: Elizabeth Russell

Printed in China

Acknowledgement

I would like to recognize and thank several people for helping me achieve to this point in my career. First, Chef David Woolums, a teacher who had more of an impact on me than any other and whose quips of infinite wisdom are still used in my own classes today. Tong Trithara, who makes some of the best food in Springfield, MO, and who helped open the door to my literary career. The Springfield News-Leader: their editors, photographers and staff, for the opportunity to share my culinary skills, and their continued belief in me even when I need to change my photo. And my many students, who continue to inspire me (more than they know) to become better at what I do, as they themselves also grow. Finally, to my daughter, Hannah, who will always prefer her macaroni and cheese out of a box; my wife, Stacy, a reformed frozen pizza aficionado who always tells me how good she thinks I am even when I doubt myself, and the dogs who have given up many walks in the park during my literary pursuits.

Chef Lou

Chef Lou and Stacy in Mexico

Forward

In the fall of 2005, when I first learned about the concept of Scallion's, the student-operated restaurant at Ozarks Technical Community College, I was introduced to Chef Lou Rice, the architect of this creative concept that blends real-world experience with academic learning. Chef Lou came to my table as I was finishing my dessert—a delicate, flaky baklava. Even at that first brief meeting, Chef embodied enthusiasm and passion for his food, just as this collection of recipes does now. Just by listening to Chef Lou talk about his dual passions for food and teaching that day, I realized just how innovative and dedicated he is.

Chef Lou's finely honed skills in culinary arts, as well as his contagious willingness to share his ideas, carried over to last spring, when I participated in a continuing education course he taught. I didn't know exactly what to expect from this course, The World Cheese Board, but I had heard Chef Lou say that it would be a lot of food. He wasn't lying! But, more importantly, what I learned that day from Chef Lou stays with me while I cook now in my own kitchen: subtle strategies, preparation techniques, and shopping hints.

Chef Lou's experiences in the classroom and as a professional chef living in the Ozarks have clearly helped him develop a fine palette and a culinary consciousness that appreciate both fine dining as well as regional cuisines. Not only can Chef Lou make both worldly dishes and less-renowned regional dishes that hold Southern or Midwest charm, but by exposing his diverse audiences to diverse cuisine, he also teaches us to value variety in our own eating.

Throughout this book, you will discover those same kinds of variety—variety not only in the varying levels of sophistication but also in the kinds of foods offered: sauces, salads, main dishes, appetizers, and side dishes. Even with this variety, though, the ingredients and directions remain accessible and focused on one audience: you, the user, the fellow cook, the collaborator.

Chef Lou's focus on the user throughout this work no doubt reflects his experience as a community college teacher as well as a local newspaper columnist who reaches out to a diverse audience every day on the job. For this reason, I am confident that novice as well as seasoned cooks will return to the recipes in this volume again and again. I know I will.

Witt Salley—Springfield, MO

6 September 2007

Contents

Chef Lou at work

Introduction

Growing up, like any kid I had heroes along the magnitude of Superman, but unlike most kids my heroes also included culinary greats Graham Kerr and Julia Child. I was simply amazed that people could be so funny and become so popular just by making food. Before I could even drive, I wanted to be the next Galloping Gourmet ala Kerr. A passion for food has always run deep within me. At an early age, food became one of my best friends; it was safety, comfort and a respite from the difficulties of daily life. While, looking back, I may have been a little too zealous at times; food has been a driving force in my life. And it didn't have to be fancy food either. Nothing gets to my heart, or stomach, like a really well made meatloaf with mashed potatoes, fried corn and homemade apple pie for dessert. Have I mentioned I love comfort food?

After a somewhat lackluster college career, I found myself in a passionless family job that barely inspired me to get out of bed. Due in great part to the fact that I had to wear a suit and tie – I suspect that the lack of my true passion, food, was my greatest unhappiness with my profession at the time. Catering the office Christmas party would have brought be much greater joy than the actual work of selling stuff no one wanted.

Finally, it became clear to me that I had to walk away from this life to preserve my own sanity and health. So off I went to culinary school. My desire to learn my new craft took me to Indianapolis, a drive of approximately 140 miles roundtrip a day, several days a week, at all hours of the day. My desire and drive, while being a positive, also made me a bit on the pushy side as I always wanted more. Completely (over) confident in my abilities, I bought a restaurant while still a student. This was the most expensive culinary education ever - and I am not talking about school tuition. Realizing restaurant ownership was not for me, at the time, I closed the restaurant after finishing school and started cooking.

During the years, I worked at a lot of the usual places, and while they left me feeling content enough, my desire for more was strong. You might have heard the saying that a chef is only as good as his last meal. Understanding this quip made me begin to think about other professions in culinary that would satisfy my passions. Teaching was my revelation. What a great career - is there anything better than talking about food all day? And an added joy for me is thriving on the experiences and successes of my students. While I love to cook, and eat, I love to teach most of all. Out of teaching comes the joy of watching others discover wonderful new flavors and foods for the first time.

I hope that you enjoy making and sampling the collected recipes in this book, but more importantly I hope that your passion for food grows just a little deeper. So read them, share them, change to fit your needs and taste but most of all just cook and enjoy.
Let's get cooking,

Chef Lou

Chef Lou

Starters

Asian Pot Stickers

48 wonton wrappers

Filling:
8 ounces Napa cabbage
3 teaspoons salt, divided
1 pound lean ground pork
1/4 cup finely chopped green
  onions
1 tablespoon white wine
1 teaspoon cornstarch
1 teaspoon sesame oil
Dash white pepper

Asian Dipping Sauce:
1/2 cup soy sauce
2 teaspoons sesame oil
2 tablespoons rice wine vinegar
1/2 teaspoon minced garlic
1 teaspoon minced green onion

Other:
2 - 4 tablespoons vegetable oil

Yields about 48

Cut the cabbage across into thin strips. Mix with 2 teaspoons salt and set aside for 5 minutes. Squeeze out the excess moisture.

In a large bowl, mix the celery, cabbage, pork, green onions, wine, cornstarch, the remaining 1 teaspoon salt, 1 teaspoon sesame oil and the white pepper.

Cut the wonton wrappers into 3-inch circles and place 1 tablespoon pork mixture in the center of the circle. Lift up the edges of the circle, dab with water to help seal and pinch 5 pleats up to create a pouch to encase the mixture. Pinch the top together.

Repeat with the remaining slices of dough and filling.

Using a bamboo steamer, or any other type of home steaming tool, steam the dumplings over water or flavored stock for about six minutes or until the dough is cooked.

Heat a nonstick skillet until very hot. Add 1 tablespoon vegetable oil, tilting the skillet to coat the sides. Place steamed dumplings in a single layer in the skillet and fry 2 minutes, or until the bottoms are golden brown.

Repeat with the rest of the dumplings. (These can be served steamed only and not fried)

To make the dipping sauce, combine all of the sauce ingredients and hold for service.

Originally printed in the News-Leader, September 2005

Blue Cheese Pear and Walnut Spread

1 can sliced pears, drained,
   chopped
1 cup cream cheese, softened
1/2 cup blue cheese crumbles
1/4 cup toasted walnuts,
   chopped
3 tablespoons green onion
1 tablespoon honey
2 tablespoons
Pinch of salt
Pinch of black pepper

Makes 4 cups

Combine all of the ingredients in a mixer and mix well.

Use as a dip, a spread or a filling.

Cheesy Artichoke Shrimp Dip

1/2 cup shredded cheddar cheese
1/2 cup grated parmesan cheese
1/2 cup Monterey Jack cheese
1/2 cup mozzarella cheese
16 ounces artichoke hearts,
   drained
1/2 cup green onions, chopped
1/2 teaspoon garlic salt
1/2 cup mayonnaise
1/4 cup sour cream
3/4 cup fresh spinach, chopped
2 cups shrimp, cooked and peeled
1 teaspoon shrimp base (optional)
1 teaspoon hot sauce
1 tablespoon lemon juice
1 cup crisp bacon, cooked
Chopped parsley

Serves 4

In a bowl, mix together all ingredients except bacon and parsley until well combined.

Pour into a casserole dish and, if desired, top with a little extra parmesan cheese.

Bake in a preheated 400 degree oven 10 minutes, or until bubbly and lightly browned.

Garnish with crumbled, crisp bacon and parsley.

Chicken Mandu

6 ounces chicken breast meat,
   finely chopped
3 ounces vegetable oil
3 tablespoons yellow onion,
   minced
3 ounces cabbage, shredded fine
2 ounces bean sprouts, roughly
   chopped
1 green onion, finely chopped
4 ounces firm tofu, mashed and
   drained
2 tablespoons hoisin sauce
2 teaspoon salt
Dash pepper
24 wonton skins
1 egg, beaten
Oil, for frying

Makes 24

Heat skillet over medium-high heat, add 4 tablespoons of oil and stir-fry meat until brown. Drain off fat and set meat aside. Heat a little more oil and sauté the onions for 3 minutes. Add the cabbage and continue cooking, stirring frequently, for another 3 minutes. Add the bean sprouts, green onion and tofu, mix well and cook for 1 to 2 minutes more. Remove pan from heat and pour cooked mixture into a colander to drain excess liquid.

In a large bowl, combine meat, vegetables, hoisin, salt, and pepper and mix well. Brush the edges of one wonton skin with a beaten egg. Place 1 teaspoon of filling mixture just above the center of skin. Fold skin in half over filling to form a triangle and press edges together to seal. Repeat with remaining skins.

Fill skillet with oil and heat to 350 degrees and deep-fry mandu until golden brown. Serve immediately.

Chile Rellenos (the healthy baked version)

4 large poblano peppers
1 tablespoon vegetable oil
6 ounces cheese of your choice
6 ounces vegetables of your
   choice (zucchini, squash, tomato,
   onion, ect.)
1 teaspoon chili powder
1/2 teaspoon garlic powder
1/2 teaspoon cumin
Salt and pepper to taste
Salsa of your choice

Serves 4

Sauté the vegetables of your choice in a little olive oil, salt, pepper, chili powder, cumin and garlic powder. Set aside

Prepare the chilies by rubbing them with the vegetable oil. Sear the skin until blackened. This can be done over an open flame like in a gas range or under the broiler that comes with your electric oven. You want the skins to be charred but not crisp. After the peppers are blackened then put the chilies in a plastic zip top bag and let sit for 15 minutes. The steam that builds up will help you remove the skin from the chilies. Peel the skin off of the chilies. Cut open a slit in the top and pull out the seeds. Leave the top with the stem attached.

Stuff the cavity with the vegetables and the cheese. Place the stuffed chilies on a baking sheet and bake in a preheated 400 degree oven for about 20 minutes.

Remove the chilies from the oven and top with the salsa then serve.

Crab Rangoon

8 ounces cream cheese
8 ounces canned crab meat,
   drained and flaked
1 tablespoon chopped red onion
2 tablespoons chopped water
   chestnuts
1/2 teaspoon Worcestershire
   sauce
1 teaspoon soy sauce
1 green onion, finely sliced
1 large clove garlic, smashed,
   peeled, and finely minced
Pinch ground black pepper
1 package wonton wrappers
   (from the local Asian market)
1 small bowl water
Oil for deep-frying, as needed

Yields 36

Combine the cream cheese and crab meat. Mix in the remaining filling ingredients one at a time.

On a flat surface, lay out a wonton wrapper in front of you so that the points go up and down and side to side. Wet the edges of the wonton.

Add one teaspoon of filling to the middle, and spread it out toward the left and right points of the wrapper so that it forms a log or rectangular shape.

Fold over the edges of the wrapper to make a triangle. Wet the edges with water and press together to seal.

Keep the completed crab rangoon covered with a damp towel or paper towel to keep them from drying out while preparing the remainder.

Heat wok, deep fryer, or heavy pan and add oil for deep-frying. When oil is ready (the temperature should be between 350 - 360 degrees), carefully slide in a few of the rangoon into the heated oil. Only put a few in at a time so you do not lower the oil temperature too much.

Deep-fry until they are golden brown, about 3 minutes, turning once. Remove with a slotted spoon and drain in a paper towel.

Serve hot with sweet and sour sauce or Chinese hot mustard.

Originally printed in the News-Leader, December 2005

Falafel

1 pound can chick peas drained
1/2 to 1 cup bread crumbs
1 egg
1 large onion, chopped
2 tablespoons parsley, finely
    chopped
1 tablespoon ground cumin
1 teaspoon dried hot red peppers
2 teaspoons garlic powder
1 teaspoon salt
1 tablespoon lemon juice
Olive oil to fry in

Serves 4

Combine chick peas, onion, parsley, beaten egg, lemon juice and spices. Mix in blender. Add bread crumbs until mixture forms a small ball without sticking to your hands.

Form chick pea mixture into small balls about one inch in diameter. Flatten patties slightly and fry until golden brown on both sides. Drain falafel balls on paper towels.

Serve individually as an appetizer or as a sandwich filling with chopped tomato, cucumber, radish, lettuce and onion in warm pita bread.

Originally printed in the News-Leader, April 2005

Gorgonzola Cheese Puffs

1 1/2 cups water
10 tablespoons butter
1 teaspoon salt
2 cups flour
5 large eggs
1 cup gorgonzola cheese,
    crumbled
Pinch of black pepper

Makes about 36 Cheese Puffs

Preheat oven to 375 degrees.
Combine the butter, salt and water in a heavy pan and bring to a boil. Add the flour and stir constantly until the flour turns into dough and pulls away from the side of the pan. Allow to cool for a few minutes then move the dough into a mixing bowl.

One at a time, add in the eggs, making sure to scrape the bowl after each addition. Finally add the gorgonzola cheese and mix well.

I use a pastry bag with a star tip but you can also use two spoons to drop small amounts of dough, around two tablespoons in size, onto a baking sheet. Keep the puffs about two inches apart. These puffs should double in size.

Bake for about 40 minutes. The puffs will be hollow so if you want to stuff with more cheese then have at it. Allow the puffs to cool before eating or stuffing.

Great Gazpacho

6 ripe tomatoes, peeled and
   chopped
1 red onion, finely chopped
1 cucumber, peeled, seeded,
   chopped
1 sweet red bell pepper (or green)
   seeded and chopped
1 stalk celery, chopped
2 tablespoons chopped fresh
   parsley
2 tablespoons chopped fresh
   chives
2 cloves garlic, minced
1/4 cup red wine vinegar
1/4 cup olive oil
3 tablespoons freshly squeezed
   lime juice
2 teaspoons sugar
Salt and fresh ground pepper, to
   taste
6 or more drops of Tabasco sauce,
   to taste
1 teaspoon Worcestershire sauce
4 cups tomato juice

Serves 4

Combine all ingredients.

Blend slightly, to desired consistency.

Place in a non-metal, non-reactive storage container, cover tightly and refrigerate overnight, allowing flavors to blend.

Originally printed in the News-Leader, July 2006

Hot Crab Dip

1/2 pound regular crabmeat
1 package (8 ounces) cream
   cheese, softened
1/2 cup mayonnaise
1 tablespoon lemon juice
2 teaspoons Worcestershire sauce
1/2 teaspoon dry mustard
1 tablespoon milk
1/4 cup chopped green onions
2 tablespoons parmesan cheese,
   shredded
2 tablespoons parmesan cheese,
   shredded
Pinch black pepper
Pinch garlic salt

Makes about 4 cups

In a large bowl add all of the ingredients except for 2 tablespoons of parmesan, and mix until smooth and creamy.

Pour into buttered 1 quart casserole. Top with remaining cheese.

Bake at 325 degrees until mixture is bubbly and browned, about 30 minutes.

Serve with crackers.

Originally printed in the News-Leader, July 2005

Hummus

1 can garbanzo beans, drained
1/2 cup tahini
   (sesame seed paste)
2 tablespoons olive oil
1/4 cup onion, diced
3 cloves garlic , smashed
1 cup olive oil
3 tablespoons fresh lemon juice
1/2 teaspoon red pepper flakes or
   more if you like

Makes 3 cups

Sauté the onion and garlic in the 2 tablespoons of olive oil until the onion is soft and just starting to brown.

Place this mix into a food processor with the drained garbanzo beans and the tahini.

Turn on the food processor and, while running, add in the olive oil and lemon juice. Add in the pepper flakes next.

If the hummus is too thick you can add in some more oil or warm water to thin it out. Let sit overnight before eating.

Mushroom Paté

1/4 cup butter
1/2 cup onion, diced
2 cloves garlic, smashed
2 pounds button mushrooms,
    chopped
1 tablespoon fresh thyme,
    chopped
2 teaspoons red pepper flakes
1/2 cup tamari or soy sauce
2 cups cream cheese,
1 tablespoon dry mustard
Salt and pepper to taste

Makes 4 cups

Sauté the onion and garlic in the butter in a heavy pan. Add in the mushrooms, pepper flakes and tamari into the pan and cook until all of the liquid is cooked away.

Remove from the heat and add in the cream cheese, mustard and thyme. Using a stick blender puree the mixture until smooth.

Adjust the seasonings with salt and pepper as needed. Allow to sit overnight before servings.

Olive Tapenade

1 cup Kalamata olives, pitted
1 cup black lives, pitted
1 cup green olives, with pimento
1/2 cup roasted red peppers
3 cloves garlic
1/4 cup capers
1/2 cup extra-virgin olive oil
2 tablespoons lemon juice
1 tablespoon fresh parsley
Black pepper to taste

Makes 5 cups

Combine all of the ingredients into a food processor. Process lightly as you don't want a paste but a finely chopped mix. Allow the flavors to come together and use as a spread or a condiment on grilled fish or chicken.

* You can just about use any olives for this, so if you cannot find a specific one, don't worry just add in more of another.

Rueben Dip

1/2 cup sauerkraut, chopped and
    drained
4 ounces cream cheese, softened
8 ounce container sour cream
1/2 cup Swiss cheese, grated
4 ounces corned beef, finely
    diced
3 tablespoons milk

Makes 4 cups

Combine and heat all ingredients except milk, in sauce, pan over low until heated through. Thin with milk if needed.

Serve with rye toast crisps or crackers.

Originally printed in the News-Leader, September 2006

Shumai

1 pound ground pork, chopped
2 cloves garlic, minced
2 teaspoons ginger, minced
2 leaves Napa cabbage, cut into
   thin strips
1/4 cup straw mushrooms,
   chopped
1/4 cup oyster sauce
1 teaspoon sugar
2 teaspoons black pepper
1 package round dumpling
   wrappers
1/4 cup water

Makes approximately 24

In a large bowl, combine pork, mushrooms, garlic, ginger, cabbage, oyster sauce, sugar, and pepper and mix well. Set aside.

Place the tips of your thumb and forefinger together to form a circle with your fingers. Center the dumpling wrapper on top of your fingers so that the center of the wrapper is in the circle of your fingers.

Spoon the filling into the wrapper and gently squeeze the sides to form the shumai.

Heat a pan of water to boiling and place a steamer pan over the water. Spray the steamer with non stick pan spray.

Place dumplings in the steamer and steam covered for 10 minutes until pork is opaque on top. Serve warm.

Originally printed in the News-Leader, April 2007

Soft Polenta with Tomato Sauce and Goat Cheese

3 cups water
2 cups milk
1 and 1/2 cups corn meal
1 teaspoon garlic powder
2 teaspoons fresh thyme, minced
2 teaspoons salt
1 teaspoon black pepper
3/4 cup parmesan cheese, grated
2 cups prepared tomato sauce
3/4 cup soft goat cheese
2 tablespoons fresh parsley,
   minced
4 tablespoons parmesan cheese,
   grated for garnish
6 tablespoons extra virgin olive
   oil

Serves 4

Bring the water and milk to a boil. Add in the seasonings. Slowly add in the corn meal stirring as you pour it in to prevent lumping. Reduce the heat to a simmer and continue to stir. Taste for enough salt and pepper.

Add in the first amount of parmesan cheese and the thyme. Polenta should be smooth and not gritty.

Pool some of the tomato sauce into 4 bowls. Spoon some of the polenta into each bowl.

Divide the goat cheese up between the four bowls and place on the polenta. Drizzle on the olive oil. Garnish with the remaining cheese and parsley

Spicy Beer Batter Fried Wings

3 pounds wings
2 tablespoons lemon juice
2 cups flour
2 teaspoons salt
2 teaspoons dry mustard
1 teaspoon garlic powder
2 teaspoons paprika
1 teaspoon pepper
1/2 teaspoon thyme
1 teaspoon cayenne
1 teaspoon baking powder
1 1/2 cups beer
1 tablespoon vegetable oil
Vegetable oil for deep-frying

Serves 4

Place wings in a shallow dish, Season with the lemon juice and salt and pepper.

In a bowl whisk together the flour, the salt, paprika, cumin, pepper, thyme, mustard, garlic, baking powder and the cayenne. Whisk in the beer and the oil until smooth. Allow the batter to rest for about 30 minutes.

In a deep kettle heat 2 inches of the oil to 350 degrees. Dip the chicken in the batter and fry it in the oil. Do a few pieces at a time so the oil temperature does not go down too much. Cook for about 4 minutes, turning to brown both sides. Remove from the oil with a slotted spoon and drain on paper towels. Return the oil to 350 degrees before adding each new batch. Season again with a little salt and serve

Originally printed in the News-Leader, January 2007

Spicy Scallop Toasts

Blackening Seasoning Mix:
2 tablespoons sugar
1/2 cup paprika
2 tablespoons garlic powder
2 tablespoons onion powder
1 teaspoon dried thyme
Pinch of salt and pepper
24 sea scallops, sliced in half
3 tablespoons minced chives

Spread:
1 cup cream cheese
1 tablespoon minced green onion
2 tablespoons roasted bell peppers
1 teaspoon garlic powder
Salt and pepper to taste
24 (1/4-inch) thick sliced rounds
   of French bread
3 tablespoons olive oil

Makes 24

Combine the blackening seasoning ingredients. Sprinkle the scallops with the seasoning powder.

In a medium high heat pan, sear the scallops on each side until they start to blacken. This will take about a minute or two on each side. When blackened set aside.

Combine the spread ingredients in a food processor.

Brush the bread with the oil and bake in a 350 degree oven for about 5 minutes to crisp.

To assemble, spread a layer of the cream cheese mix on top of the toasted bread round. Place two of the scallop halves on top of the cheese and garnish with some minced chives.

Steamed Shrimp Stuffed Dumplings

50 wonton skins
25 medium-sized shrimp, shelled, deveined
12 ounces shrimp, shelled and coarsely minced
8 ounces ground pork, finely chopped
1/4 teaspoon pepper
1/4 teaspoon salt
1/4 teaspoon sugar
1 egg white, lightly beaten
1 teaspoon hot chili oil
Nonstick pan coating

Marinade:
2 tablespoons green onion, minced
1 teaspoon cornstarch
2 tablespoons Chinese rice wine
1/2 tablespoon sesame oil
1 tablespoon soy sauce
1 teaspoon sugar
1 teaspoon ground ginger
1/2 teaspoon salt
1/2 teaspoon pepper

Makes 25

Mix all the marinade ingredients together in a bowl.

Combine the minced shrimp and pork and pour the marinade liquid to mix thoroughly. Marinate for at least 30 minutes. Season whole shrimp with pepper, sugar and salt and set aside.

Place a spoonful of the shrimp and pork filling onto the middle of a wonton. Place one shrimp on top of the filling. Take another wonton skin, brushed lightly with egg white, and place over the shrimp and filling.

Seal the two wonton skins together by lightly pressing them. Use a biscuit cutter to cut the dumpling into a round shape.

Spray a bamboo steamer with a nonstick pan spray to prevent the dumplings from sticking.

Arrange the wrapped shrimp dumplings on the bamboo steamer and cover the top.

Allow to steam for approximately 8 minutes.
Serve immediately.

Originally printed in the News-Leader, April 2007

Stuffed Turkey Mushrooms

1 tablespoon olive oil
1 small onion, diced
3 teaspoons apple cider vinegar
1/2 teaspoon fresh parsley,
  chopped
1 teaspoon ground sage
1/2 teaspoon mustard powder
1 teaspoon garlic powder
1/2 teaspoon red pepper flakes
1 teaspoon salt
1/2 teaspoon pepper
1 pound 93% lean ground turkey
1 pound large button mushrooms,
  stems removed
1 tablespoon Worcestershire sauce
1/2 cup cream cheese, softened
1/2 cup fontina cheese, finely
  shredded

Serves 4

Preheat oven to 400 degrees.
Sauté the onion in the oil until the onion is softened and just starting to turn brown, then remove from heat and cool.

Mix together parsley, sage, mustard powder, salt, pepper, red pepper flakes and garlic.

Place turkey in a medium bowl and mix together with the spices. Stir in the vinegar, Worcestershire, the two cheeses and the cooked onions.

Season the mushroom caps with a little salt and pepper. Use a piping bag to pipe the filling into the cap. If you have no bag, use a pair of spoons.

Bake the stuffed mushrooms until they begin to soften and the cheese is melted and golden, about 30 minutes.

Sweet-Sour Chicken Wings

2 pounds chicken wings
1 cup ketchup
3 tablespoons orange marmalade
1 tablespoon honey
2 teaspoons soy sauce
2 teaspoons minced ginger
2 teaspoons hot pepper sauce
4 garlic cloves, smashed and
  minced
1 teaspoon salt
1/2 cup pineapple juice
  (more as needed)

Serves 4

Blend all ingredients except chicken.

Place 3/4 of sauce in bowl.

Roll wings in sauce; remove wings to sheet tray with a drain tray on top.

Bake at 325 degrees for 20 minutes.

Remove from the oven and sauté the wings in the remaining sauce for about 3 minutes.

Originally printed in the News-Leader, January 2007

Tangy Goat Cheese and Red Pepper Dip

One 3- to 4-ounce jar of roasted
   red bell peppers
2 green onions, minced
1 tablespoon capers
1 teaspoon fresh minced garlic
4 ounces cream cheese
12 ounces soft goat cheese
1 teaspoon grainy mustard
Salt and pepper to taste

Makes approximately 2 cups

Place peppers, green onions, capers and garlic in a food processor and pulse until mixture is smooth. Add goat cheese, cream cheese and mustard and pulse to blend.

Season with salt and pepper, cover and chill before serving with vegetables and crunchy bread sticks.

Vermont Cheddar Cheese Cheesecake
with Apple Cider Mustard

3/4 cup onion, diced small
1 tablespoon oil
24 ounces cream cheese
1 tablespoon cornstarch
1 teaspoon dry mustard
Pinch salt
6 ounces white Vermont cheddar
   cheese, finely chopped
4 eggs
3/4 cup heavy cream
2 teaspoons McElhenny's green
   hot sauce

Crust:
2 cups ground Ritz style crackers
3 tablespoons butter, melted
1/4 cup walnuts, toasted and
   crushed

Apple Cider Mustard:
1 cup Creole mustard
1 tablespoon apple jelly
4 tablespoons apple cider

Makes 12 servings

Sweat the onions on medium heat until they caramelize to a nice golden brown, not burnt, and let cool. Beat the cream cheese, cornstarch, mustard and salt in a stand mixer until fluffy, then add in the cooked onions. Add in the cheddar cheese and beat on high to combine. Lower the speed and add in the eggs one at a time.

Stop the mixer and scrape the bottom of the bowl and the sides. Add in the heavy cream. Season with salt and pepper.

Pour into prepared crust and bake at 325 degrees for 10 minutes. Reduce the heat and bake for another 30 minutes at 250 degrees. Cool for service.

Crust:
Combine all ingredients and pat into a 10-inch cake pan. Crust should be on the bottom only and not the sides.

Apple Cider Mustard:
Combine all ingredients and refrigerate until ready to use.

Salads & Salad Dressings

All Purpose Asian Vinaigrette

1/4 cup low-sodium soy sauce
2 tablespoons vegetable oil
2 tablespoons rice vinegar
2 tablespoons sweet rice cooking
  wine
4 teaspoons fresh lime juice
4 teaspoons fresh lemon juice
3 teaspoons sugar
2 teaspoons fresh ginger, grated
2 teaspoons sesame oil
2 cloves garlic, minced
2 tablespoons green onion minced

Makes about 1/2 cup or
  4 servings

Combine all ingredients in small bowl and whisk together.

This dressing would make a good marinade for pork or chicken or can be tossed into a bowl of cold noodles with veggies for a great quick summer salad.

Apple and Pear Slaw

3 cups chopped cabbage
1 unpeeled red pear, cored and
  chopped
1 unpeeled Granny Smith apple,
  cored and chopped
1 carrot, grated
1/2 cup finely chopped red bell
  pepper
1/2 cup toasted walnuts
2 green onions, finely chopped
1/3 cup mayonnaise
1/3 cup brown sugar
1 tablespoon lemon juice, or to
  taste

8-10 servings

In a large bowl, combine cabbage, apple, pear, carrot, red bell pepper, nuts and green onions.

In a small bowl, mix together mayonnaise, brown sugar and lemon juice.

Pour dressing over salad, toss and chill.

Asian Cole Slaw

1 teaspoon fresh ginger,
    grated fine
1/2 cup rice wine vinegar
1 tablespoon soy sauce
1 lime, juiced
2 tablespoons honey
2 tablespoons sesame oil
1/2 cup peanut butter
1 head Napa cabbage, sliced thin
1 red bell pepper, julienned fine
1 yellow bell pepper, julienned fine
1 carrot, grated fine
1/2 cup slivered almonds
3 green onions, cut on the bias
1 tablespoon toasted sesame seeds
1/2 teaspoon black pepper

8-10 servings

In a small bowl or food processor combine ginger, vinegar, soy sauce, lime juice, oil, honey and peanut butter.

In a large bowl, combine all other ingredients and then toss with dressing.

Chill and serve.

Originally printed in the News-Leader, August 2005

Asian Pea Salad

1 cup sugar snap peas
1/2 cup snow peas
1/2 cup shelled fresh green peas
1 tablespoon sesame seeds,
    toasted
1 tablespoon rice vinegar
1 tablespoon sesame oil
1 teaspoon fresh garlic, minced
3 tablespoons green onion, sliced
2 tablespoons honey
3 teaspoons soy sauce
6 cups pea shoots

Serves 4

In a pan of boiling salted water cook sugar snap peas 2 minutes.

Add snow peas and green peas and cook 1 minute.

Drain peas in a colander and rinse under cold water.

In a small bowl whisk together sesame seeds, vinegar, oil, honey, garlic, green onion and soy sauce.

In a bowl toss pea shoots and peas with dressing.

Asian Style Asparagus and Crab Salad

Dressing:
Combine all ingredients; mix well. Set aside.

Salad:
Steam asparagus until tender-crisp. Drain and let cool. Cut crab into bite-size pieces. Combine asparagus and crab in a large bowl; add remaining ingredients and toss gently.

Pour salad dressing over all and toss to coat. Serve immediately.

Originally printed in the News-Leader, May 2005

Dressing:
2 tablespoons olive oil
2 tablespoons rice vinegar
2 tablespoons sugar
1 tablespoon orange juice concentrate
1 tablespoon lime juice
1 tablespoon dark sesame oil

Salad:
2 cups cut-up fresh asparagus, blanched
12 ounces crab meat (fresh or canned) or imitation crab
10 ounces romaine lettuce and red leaf lettuce mixed
2 tablespoons diced red onion
3 button mushrooms (sliced)
1 cup sliced seedless cucumber

Serves 4

Avocado Vinaigrette

Use this vinaigrette to dress up grilled tuna or salmon.

Combine all ingredients in a blender and process until smooth. Serve immediately.

Originally printed in the News-Leader, August 2005

1 medium avocado, peeled and pitted
3 tablespoons lime juice
2 tablespoons rice wine vinegar
2/3 cup vegetable stock
1/2 teaspoon salt
1 clove garlic, minced
1 green onion, minced
1 teaspoon honey
Pinch of pepper

Makes about 10 servings

Basic French Dressing (a simple vinaigrette)

1/4 cup vinegar (your choice but
  red wine vinegar is a good
  starter)
3/4 cup oil (olive oil preferred)
1 clove garlic mashed
1 teaspoon oregano
Salt and pepper to taste

Makes 1 cup and serves 8

Dissolve the salt in the vinegar.

Add the oil, pepper and seasonings and whisk or process to combine.

Blood Orange Vinaigrette

6 tablespoons blood orange juice
2 tablespoons rice vinegar
1/2 teaspoon Dijon mustard
2 teaspoons honey
  (orange blossom if possible)
1 teaspoon fresh rosemary,
  chopped
1 teaspoon green onion, minced
Pinch each of salt and pepper to
  taste
1/2 cup salad or light olive oil

Makes 1 1/2 cups

In a blender, whisk up the juice, vinegar, mustard, honey, rosemary, green onion and salt and pepper.

Slowly, with the blender running, add the oil and blend until emulsified.

Taste; it should taste slightly acidic but not sharp, and well seasoned.

Serve this dressing on a salad of baby greens, roasted beets and shrimp.

Cantaloupe Spinach Salad

4 cups spinach leaves, washed
  and stemmed
1 cup cantaloupe, peeled and
  diced
1 cup avocado, sliced
1/4 cup red bell pepper, diced
4 red onion rings
2 tablespoons fresh mint leaves,
  shredded
2 tablespoons walnuts, toasted,
  and chopped

Serves 2

Divide spinach between 2 serving plates. Arrange half of the cantaloupe and half of the avocado over the spinach.

Sprinkle with diced red pepper, nuts and fresh mint and top with red onion rings.

Drizzle with lemon poppy seed dressing (see page 33) right before serving.

Originally printed in the News-Leader, July 2006

Chicken Salad with Apple and Walnut Vinaigrette

4 boneless skinless chicken
 breasts

Marinade:
2 cups apple juice or cider
1 clove garlic, minced
1 green onion, minced
1 tablespoon coarse grain mustard

Dressing:
4 tablespoons walnuts, toasted
1/3 cup walnut oil
1/2 cup apple cider vinegar
3 tablespoons shallots, minced
1 clove garlic, smashed
1 teaspoon coarse grain mustard
1 tablespoon honey
2 tablespoons chives, minced
2 tablespoons apple cider vinegar
Salt and pepper to taste

2 Fuji apples
1/2 cup red onion, sliced
4 cups mixed salad greens
1/4 cup dried cranberries
4 tablespoons walnuts, toasted

Serves 4

Marinate the chicken breast for four hours or overnight in the marinade.

In large bowl, combine dressing ingredients. Drain the chicken and grill or saut   the chicken until done.

Core the apples and cut into bite-size pieces. Add apples and onion to mixed baby greens.

Add dressing and mix to coat, then place salad ingredients on four plates.

Slice the chicken breast and place on top of the greens and garnish with dried cranberries and more walnuts.

Originally printed in the News-Leader, October 2006

Creamy Crab Pasta Salad

12 ounces medium shell pasta
1 pound cooked crab meat
1 1/2 cups diced sweet red peppers
1 cup diced sweet green peppers
3/4 cup diced red onions
1/4 cup diced celery
1/2 cup chopped green onions

Dressing:
1 cup mayonnaise
2 teaspoons Old Bay seasoning
2 tablespoons lemon juice
2 teaspoons crushed garlic
1 teaspoon Dijon mustard
2 teaspoons fresh minced parsley

Serves 4

Cook pasta in boiling water according to package instructions or until firm to the bite. Rinse with cold water.

Drain and place in serving bowl. Add all vegetables and crab to the pasta.

Add all of the dressing ingredients together in a bowl and mix until smooth. Toss into the crab/vegetable mix and chill for service.

Curried Tuna Salad

3 cans tuna, drained
3 green onions, chopped
1 Granny Smith apple, chopped
1/4 cup celery, chopped
1/2 red bell pepper, chopped
3/4 cup mayonnaise
1 tablespoon yellow curry powder
2 tablespoons honey
1 tablespoon stone-ground
   mustard
Salt and pepper to taste

Serves 4

Combine all ingredients and season to taste.

Refrigerate for a few hours then serve.

Originally printed in the News-Leader, March 2006

Dried Cranberry Poppy Seed

3/4 cup sugar
1/2 cup dried cranberries
2 tablespoons onion, minced
1 teaspoon dry mustard
1/3 cup apple cider vinegar
1 cup light olive oil
1 tablespoon poppy seeds
Water as needed for thinning

Makes about 1 2/3 cups
    or 12 to 16 servings

In a blender, combine sugar, salt and dry mustard. Turn the blender to medium speed and add in the vinegar. Beat at medium speed while gradually adding the oil.

Add in the dried cranberries and continue to blend until thickened, adding in a little water if the dressing is too thick.

Stop blender and stir in poppy seeds. Store covered in refrigerator and shake well before using.

Fat Free Raspberry Vinaigrette

1 cup fresh raspberries
1/2 cup raspberry vinegar
2 tablespoons honey
1 tablespoon fresh mint leaves,
    finely chopped
Salt and pepper to taste

Makes 10 servings

Place berries in a container and mash. Add vinegar, honey and mint, cover with lid, and shake to dissolve sugar. Stir in additional honey (up to another tablespoon or more) if necessary, to smooth out the vinegar flavor.

Originally printed in the News-Leader, August 2005

Gingered Spam Noodle Salad

1 can Spam, sliced matchstick size
1/2 tablespoon fresh ginger,
    finely minced
4 tablespoons red onion,
    finely chopped
2 green onions, minced
1 teaspoon garlic powder
2 teaspoons sesame oil
2 tablespoons soy sauce
3 tablespoons lime juice
1 teaspoon lime zest
4 tablespoons salad oil
1/2 teaspoon red pepper flakes
6 cups Asian style wheat noodles,
    cooked and drained

Serves 4

Combine all ingredients in a container and allow to marinate refrigerated overnight.

Stir occasionally while marinating.

Originally printed in the News-Leader, October 2005

HARTER HOUSE ~
FAMOUS FOR OUR MEATS

The Finest Quality Dry Aged Meat,
Aged Cheese & Specialty Items

Welcome to Harter House Supermarket, a company dedicated to offering the finest ingredients for your dining pleasure. *Our philosophy is simple... we only sell the highest quality products.* You'll see and taste the difference when you experience our old-fashioned neighborhood market.

Quality meats and great service.

Harter House Supermarkets

Horseradish Vinaigrette

1 cup vegetable oil
1/2 cup apple cider vinegar
1/2 cup white sugar
2 tablespoons prepared
   horseradish
1 tablespoon Dijon mustard
1 teaspoon lemon juice
1 clove garlic, crushed
1 teaspoon salt

Makes 2 1/2 cups

Blend all ingredients and serve.

Originally printed in the News-Leader, October 2006

Hot Bacon Vinaigrette

5 slices bacon
3 tablespoons apple cider vinegar
1 tablespoon lemon juice
2 teaspoons white sugar
1/2 teaspoon ground black pepper
2 tablespoons green onion,
   minced
1/2 teaspoon dry mustard
Salt to taste

Makes 3/4 cup
   or 3 to 6 servings

Place bacon in a large, deep skillet. Cook over medium high heat until evenly brown. Remove the bacon from skillet, crumble and set aside.

To the hot bacon drippings, add the onion, vinegar, lemon juice, sugar, mustard and pepper. Stir over medium heat until hot. Add in the bacon and serve.

Lemon Poppy Seed Dressing

4 tablespoons vegetable oil
3 tablespoons lemon juice
2 tablespoons honey
1/2 teaspoon poppy seeds
1 teaspoon green onion, minced
Pinch mustard powder
Pinch salt and pepper

Serves 2

With a whisk or electric mixer, combine all ingredients until emulsified. Just before serving, whisk again.

Originally printed in the News-Leader, July 2006

Mango Slaw

2 tablespoons honey
1/4 cup Hellman's mayonnaise
3 tablespoons lime juice
1/2 teaspoon salt
1/4 teaspoon pepper
1 cup red cabbage, shredded
2 cups savoy cabbage, shredded
1/2 cup carrots, peeled and
  julienned
1 ripe mango, peeled, seeded and
  cut into 1/2 inch pieces

Serves 4

In a small bowl, mix together the honey, mayonnaise, lime juice, salt and pepper.

In a large bowl, place the red cabbage, savoy cabbage, and carrots; toss well to mix. Add the honey-lime mixture and mango to cabbage and toss gently to mix.

Mozzarella Tomato Salad

1 pound tomatoes, large, red and
  yellow mixed, very ripe
4 ounces mozzarella cheese,
  shredded (if you can get fresh
  mozzarella then use it)
8 fresh basil leaves
1/2 teaspoon fresh thyme leaves
1/2 of a small red onion, cut into
  very thin half moon slices.
1/4 cup sliced black olives
2 tablespoons extra virgin olive
  oil
1 teaspoon lemon juice
1 clove of garlic, mashed
4 tablespoons parmesan cheese,
  grated for garnish
2 tablespoons pine nuts, toasted
  for garnish
Salt and pepper to taste
Red and green leaf lettuce

Serves 4

Combine the olive oil, lemon juice, mashed garlic, salt and pepper and set aside.

Arrange a layer of leaf lettuce on a serving platter.

Slice tomatoes crosswise into 1/4-inch-thick slices.

Arrange the slices on top of the leaf lettuce.

Toss on the sliced red onion and the black olives.

Roll up the basil leaves into a small tube and cut into thin strips and top each tomato with basil.

Sprinkle the mozzarella on top.

Garnish with pine nuts and parmesan cheese.

Mustard Grilled Salmon Salad

1 pound salmon fillet, cut into
   4 pieces
2 tablespoons olive oil
1/2 red onion, sliced thick
1 red bell pepper, sliced
1 zucchini, sliced
1 summer squash, sliced
2 cups penne pasta
3 cups fresh spinach
1 tablespoon chopped fresh dill
3/4 cup prepared honey mustard
   salad dressing
Salt and pepper to taste

Serves 4

Heat the grill. Brush salmon with olive oil and place on grill. Toss the vegetables with 1 tablespoon of olive oil and place in a grill basket.

Grill the salmon and vegetables 4 to 6 inches from medium coals until the salmon is medium and the vegetables are crisp-tender.

Cook and drain pasta. Mix pasta and about 1/4 cup of the dressing. Add in the grilled vegetables and spinach.

Divide among four plates and top with salmon.

Drizzle with remaining dressing and sprinkle with dill.

Originally printed in the News-Leader, June 2006

Peachy Duck Salad with Blue Cheese and Almonds

12 ounces mixed greens
3 ounces red onion, thinly sliced
8 ounces fresh or frozen sliced
   peaches
12 ounces roast duck breast,
   cooked and shredded
6 ounces almonds, toasted
2 ounces blue cheese
1/3 cup cider vinegar
2 tablespoons honey
3/4 cup light olive oil
2 tablespoons peach preserves
1 teaspoon dry mustard
1 teaspoon dried thyme

Serves 4

Great for using up any leftover duck.

For the dressing combine all ingredients in a blender or food processor and hold for service.

Divide salad ingredients into four servings.

Place greens on a cold plate.

Place peach slices on the greens and top with the shredded duck.

Top with the onion slices, toasted almonds and cheese crumbles.

Drizzle the salads with the dressing and serve.

Originally printed in the News-Leader, November 2005

Raspberry Balsamic Vinaigrette

3 tablespoons balsamic vinegar
1 tablespoon honey
3 tablespoons seedless raspberry
  preserves
2 tablespoons olive oil
Salt and pepper to taste

Makes approximately 1 cup

Heat the vinegar and honey together in a small saucepan until the honey dissolves. Transfer to a small bowl and whisk in the preserves and olive oil.

For a delicious change try using walnut oil in this recipe.

Real 1000 Island Dressing

1 cup mayonnaise
1/4 cup chili sauce
1/8 cup pimiento-stuffed green
  olives, finely chopped
2 tablespoons green bell pepper,
  finely chopped
1 green onion, finely chopped
1 hard boiled egg, peeled and
  finely chopped

Makes 1 1/2 cups

Combine all ingredients in a bowl, mix well and refrigerate until ready to use.

Originally printed in the News-Leader, September 2005

Refrigerator Salad

1 head of red leaf lettuce, torn
1/2 cup roasted red bell pepper,
  diced
1/2 cup green pepper, diced
1 red onion, chopped
1 package frozen baby green
  peas, slightly thawed
1 cup mayonnaise
2 tablespoons Dijon or Creole
  mustard
2 teaspoons honey
4 ounces cheddar cheese, grated
8 slices bacon, crumbled

Serves 4

Layer the first 5 ingredients in a glass bowl in order of listing.

Combine mayonnaise, mustard and honey.

Drizzle over the first five ingredients.

Sprinkle on cheese, then bacon.

Cover and refrigerate overnight. Toss lightly just before serving.

Originally printed in the News-Leader, May 2007

Roasted Beet Salad with Feta, Walnuts and Orange Walnut Vinaigrette

Orange Walnut Vinaigrette:
1 tablespoon apple cider vinegar
1 1/2 cups fresh orange juice
2 tablespoons balsamic vinegar
1 teaspoon minced fresh thyme
*   leaves*
1/2 teaspoon grated orange zest
1 shallot, peeled and minced
1/3 cup walnut oil
1/3 cup extra-virgin olive oil
Salt and freshly ground black
*   pepper*

Beet Salad:
1 ounce whole toasted walnuts
1 pound fresh beets
Salt and pepper to taste
3 ounces feta cheese
3 ounces mixed baby greens

Serves 4

In a saucepan bring orange juice to a boil. Reduce heat to low and continue simmering until 1/3 cup of juice remains, 10 to 15 minutes. Remove from heat and cool to room temperature.

Transfer reduced juice to a mixing bowl and whisk in apple cider vinegar, balsamic vinegar, thyme, orange zest and shallot. Whisking continuously, slowly drizzle in the walnut and olive oils to form a thick emulsion.

Season to taste with salt and pepper, cover and refrigerate until needed.

Beet Salad:
Wash beets thoroughly. With a sharp knife, trim off greens, leaving short sections of stem attached and taking care not to cut into the roots.

Bake the beets on a tray in a preheated 375 degree oven until they are tender through the middle. While still warm, hold each beet with a few layers of paper towel to protect your hand and, with a small, sharp knife, peel off skins and trim stems and root tips.

Cut each beet into 4 to 6 bite-sized wedges and place in a mixing bowl with 3 tablespoons vinaigrette. Toss well and divide among 4 chilled salad plates.

Crumble goat cheese over beets and sprinkle with walnuts. Put greens in mixing bowl and add 1 tablespoon vinaigrette. Toss well and place a cluster of greens on top of each serving. Drizzle 1/2 tablespoon vinaigrette around each plate.

Originally printed in the News-Leader, April 2004

Simple Goat Cheese and Fruit Salad

2 cups red leaf lettuce - rinsed, dried and torn
4 tablespoons raspberry walnut vinaigrette
1/2 cup seedless red grapes, halved
4 tablespoons crumbled goat cheese
2 tablespoons pecans, chopped and toasted
1 Granny Smith apple, cored and diced

Serves 2

Toss all ingredients with dressing in a mixing bowl, plate and serve.

Originally printed in the News-Leader, August 2006

Smoked-Chicken and Cranberry Salad

1/2 cup dried cranberries
1/4 cup mayonnaise
1 tablespoon fresh orange juice
3 cups sliced smoked chicken breast, cut into 1/2-inch pieces
1/3 cup sliced almonds with skins, toasted and cooled
1 celery rib, thinly sliced
2 green onions sliced thin
1 tablespoon honey
Salt and pepper to taste

Makes 4 main-course servings

Soak cranberries in a bowl of warm water 15 minutes, then drain well and chop.

Whisk together mayonnaise and orange juice in a medium bowl, then add cranberries, remaining ingredients, and salt and pepper to taste, tossing to coat.

Originally printed in the News-Leader, November 2005

Strawberry Vinaigrette

1 cup olive oil
1/2 pint strawberries, hulled
3 tablespoons balsamic vinegar
1/2 teaspoon salt
1/4 teaspoon pepper
1/4 teaspoon dried tarragon, crumbled
2 tablespoons honey

16 servings

Combine the olive oil, strawberries, vinegar, salt, pepper, tarragon and honey in a food processor. Process until all the berries are puréed and smooth.

Toss with a salad of greens, berries, oranges and almonds.

Originally printed in the News-Leader, August 2005

Soups & Sandwiches

Avgolemono / Greek Lemon Soup

2 cups chicken broth
1 cup water
3 tablespoons lemon juice
2 large eggs, lightly beaten
1 cup hot cooked long grain rice
1/2 teaspoon salt
1/8 teaspoon white pepper
6 lemon slices

Serves 4

Heat broth and water in medium saucepan over medium high heat. Gradually add hot broth mixture and lemon juice to eggs, stirring constantly with a whisk. Return mixture to pan.

Cook over medium heat until slightly thick (about 15 minutes), stirring constantly. Remove from heat; stir in rice, season and serve with a lemon slice.

Originally printed in the News-Leader, February 2005

Bay Scallop Roll

1 tablespoon olive oil
1 tablespoon butter
2 teaspoons garlic, chopped
1 tablespoon green onions, chopped
2 tablespoons fresh parsley, chopped
1 pound bay scallops
2 tablespoons lemon juice
2 tablespoons white wine
2 tablespoons mayonnaise
4 soft rolls

Makes 2 to 4 servings

In a sauté pan over medium high heat, heat the olive oil and butter.

Add the garlic and cook for 1 minute.

Add the herbs and cook for 30 seconds.

Add the scallops and cook for 1 minute.

Add the lemon and wine and cook for another 2 to 3 minutes, until the scallops are just cooked, but not overcooked.

Remove from the heat and stir in the mayonnaise. Serve on soft rolls.

Originally printed in the News-Leader, July 2005

Caribbean Turkey Burgers with Grilled Pineapple Chutney

1 ripe fresh pineapple, peeled,
  cored and cut into 1/2-inch
  thick slices (You can use canned
  pineapple rings if desired)
1 large onion, peeled and sliced
1/3 cup brown sugar
1/4 cup apple cider-wine vinegar
1 tablespoon orange peel, grated
1 tablespoon fresh ginger, grated
1/2 teaspoon allspice
1/4 cup red bell pepper, minced
16-ounce package extra-lean
  ground turkey
1 1/2 teaspoons jerk seasoning
Salt and pepper to taste
4 hamburger buns
Leaf lettuce leaves

Makes 4 servings

To make the chutney, grill pineapple and onions on lightly oiled grill for about 5 minutes over medium-high heat so they will be lightly charred. Allow to cool.

Finely chop pineapple and onion and place in a medium saucepan with brown sugar, vinegar, orange peel, ginger and allspice; stir well. Bring to a boil; reduce heat and simmer for 30 minutes. Add bell pepper and cook for 10 minutes more; let cool.

In a medium bowl, stir together the ground turkey, 1/2 cup pineapple chutney, jerk seasoning and pepper. Shape into 4 large flat patties.

Grill over medium heat for 5 to 8 minutes per side or until cooked through. Serve on toasted buns lined with lettuce leaves. Place a heaping spoonful of chutney on top of each burger.

Originally printed in the News-Leader, May 2007

Cincinnati Chili

3 onions, chopped
6 garlic cloves, minced
3 tablespoons oil
4 pounds ground beef
1/3 cup chili powder
2 tablespoons paprika
2 teaspoons powdered cumin
1 teaspoon coriander
1 teaspoon allspice
1 teaspoon dried oregano
1/2 teaspoon cayenne pepper
1/2 teaspoon clove
1/4 teaspoon mace
1 bay leaf
3 cups water
1 can (16-ounce.) tomato sauce
2 tablespoons wine vinegar
2 tablespoons molasses
Salt and pepper to taste

Serves 4

In a large pot, sauté onions and garlic in oil over medium heat until onions are soft. Add beef and stir until browned. Add spices, water, tomato sauce, vinegar and molasses. Simmer uncovered for two hours, stirring occasionally.

The code for ordering Cincinnati chili is listed below:

One-way: chili only (but never ordered this way).
Two-way: spaghetti topped with chili only.
Three-way: add shredded cheddar cheese.
Four-way: add chopped onions.
Five-way: add beans.

Originally printed in the News-Leader, October 2004

Classic Chicago Dog

8 all beef hot dogs, not skinless
8 poppy seeded hot dog buns
2 tomatoes
16 sport peppers or similar
  pickled peppers
1/2 cup onion, chopped
1/2 cup sweet pickle relish
1 tablespoon celery salt
8 dill pickles

Serves 4

Cut tomatoes into thin slices, then cut in half to make half circles. Simmer the hot dogs in water until just warmed through. In Chicago, they call this water bathing.

Open hot dog buns and grill for 1 minute cut side down.

Assemble dogs by placing 2 slices of tomato on the bun, then the hot dog, and then the peppers. Now top with onions and relish. Sprinkle on some celery salt.

You can now top with mustard but for a real Chicago dog never use ketchup.

Originally printed in the News-Leader, June 2007

Cold Plum Soup

16-ounce can purple plums with
  syrup
1 cup water
2/3 cup sugar
1 cinnamon stick
1/4 teaspoon white pepper
Pinch salt
1 cup sour cream
1/2 cup heavy cream
1/2 cup dry red wine
1 tablespoon cornstarch
2 tablespoons lemon juice
1 teaspoon grated lemon rind

Serves 4

Pit and chop plums, combine with the plum syrup in a saucepan. Add water, sugar, cinnamon, salt and pepper. Bring to a boil, reduce heat and simmer 5 minutes, stirring occasionally.

Mix wine and heavy cream with cornstarch, add to mixture and cook until thickened. Stir in lemon juice and rind, remove from heat.

Place 1/2 cup soup in small bowl, whisk in sour cream. Stir mix back into the soup pan until smooth. Chill at least 4 hours.

Garnish with dollops of sour cream and sprinkle with cinnamon.

* This soup can be made with fresh plums but we have found the canned versions taste just as good in this soup.

Originally printed in the News-Leader, July 2005

Cold Tomato Puree Soup

3 pounds ripe tomatoes, peeled
   and quartered
2 - 4 tablespoons fresh lemon
   juice
1 tablespoon finely chopped
   scallion greens
2 teaspoons finely grated fresh
   lemon zest
1 teaspoon sugar
Pinch of dried thyme, crumbled
Pinch of dried marjoram, crumbled
1 teaspoon salt
1/4 teaspoon black pepper
1 cup sour cream
Fresh parsley leaves for garnish

Makes 6 servings

Purée tomatoes in batches in a blender until smooth, then force purée through a sieve into a large bowl, discarding seeds.

Stir in lemon juice to taste, scallion, zest, sugar, thyme, marjoram, salt and pepper.

Chill soup until cold, about 1 hour.

Ladle soup into bowls and top with dollops of sour cream.

Corn Chowder

1/2 pound bacon
1 large onion, chopped
2 garlic cloves, minced
1/2 cup celery, chopped
1/2 cup carrot, chopped
1/2 cup red bell pepper, chopped
2 (14-ounce) cans chicken broth
4 cups potatoes, peeled and diced
3 cups half-and-half
4 cups fresh or frozen corn kernels
2 teaspoons fresh thyme, chopped
Salt and pepper to taste
Garnishes: bacon bits and
   chopped green onions

Serves 4

In a heavy stock pot, over medium-high heat, cook the bacon until crispy, about 8 minutes. Remove the bacon and hold for later use.

Add the onion, garlic, celery, bell pepper and carrot and sauté until tender. Stir in the chicken broth, potatoes, salt and pepper. Bring to a boil and reduce the heat. Simmer for 30 to 45 minutes or until the potatoes are tender.

Stir in the half-and-half and corn. Cook for 25 to 30 minutes or until of the desired consistency, stirring frequently. Add in the thyme.

Ladle into soup bowls. Garnish with bacon bits and chopped green onions.

For a change of taste, substitute clam juice for the chicken stock and substitute fresh chunks of boneless catfish for the corn. You can get fresh catfish year round and its firmness makes it perfect for this hearty fare.

Originally printed in the News-Leader, February 2004

Cream of Lettuce Soup

1 cup yellow onion, chopped
1 garlic clove, chopped
3 tablespoons butter
3/4 teaspoon ground coriander
3/4 teaspoon salt
1/4 teaspoon black pepper
3/4 cup potato, peeled and diced
8 cups leaf lettuce leaves
   including ribs, coarsely chopped
3 cups light chicken stock
1 cup heavy cream
1 tablespoon butter

Serves 4

Melt butter in a heavy pot and sauté the onions and garlic for about 3 minutes. Add in the coriander, salt, and pepper and cook, stirring, 1 minute.

Stir in potato, lettuce and light chicken stock and bring to a boil, then reduce heat and simmer, covered, until the potatoes are very tender, about 10 minutes.

Purée the soup in batches with a blender and then return it to the pot. Add in the cream and bring the puréed soup to a simmer, then whisk in remaining tablespoon of butter and salt and pepper to taste.

Originally printed in the News-Leader, May 2007

Cream of Tomato

8 bacon slices
1/2 cup carrots, diced
3/4 cup onions, diced
1/2 cup celery, diced
3 garlic cloves, diced
4 cups tomato, diced
4 cups tomato puree
2 cups ketchup
5 cups chicken stock
2 cups heavy cream
Salt and pepper to taste

Serves 4

Sauté bacon till crisp and remove, reserving the grease.

Sauté the carrots, onion and celery for 5 minutes. Add in the remaining ingredients except for the cream and bring to a simmer.

Simmer for 20 minutes, reduce the heat and add in the cream. Season to taste.

Originally printed in the News-Leader, July 2006

Curried Ginger Carrot Soup

1/2 cup green onion, chopped
1 small onion, cut in 4 pieces
1 1/2 pounds carrots, cut in
   1-inch pieces
3 tablespoon fresh ginger, peeled,
   grated
2 teaspoons yellow curry powder
1 (14-ounce) can chicken broth
1 (13.5-ounce) can unsweetened
   coconut milk + extra for garnish
1 tablespoon lime juice
3 tablespoons honey
Fresh chives, minced for garnish
Salt and pepper to taste

Makes about 6 servings

Place green onions, onion pieces and carrots in a food processor. Processe until the vegetables are coarsely chopped.

Combine chopped vegetables, grated ginger, curry powder and chicken broth in a large saucepan. Bring to a boil and simmer for about 20 minutes until the vegetables are very soft.

Strain vegetables and reserve the liquid. Add vegetables to food processor in batches and process until smooth. Add the vegetables, the vegetable liquid, coconut milk, honey and lime and stir until mixed thoroughly. Strain through a sieve to make a nice smooth texture.

Refrigerate until well chilled. Adjust seasonings as needed.

This soup can be served hot or cold.

Originally printed in the News-Leader, May 2007

Eggplant Sandwich

1 loaf Italian bread
2 teaspoons garlic powder
3 tablespoons butter
1 unpeeled eggplant, cut crosswise
   into rounds about 1/2 inch
1 jar roasted red bell pepper,
   sliced
1 onion, sliced thin
Fresh herbs (basil or whatever
   you prefer)
4 slices provolone cheese, sliced
4 tablespoons parmesan cheese,
   shredded
8 tomato slices
4 tablespoons creamy Italian
   dressing

Serves 4

Arrange eggplant slices in a single layer on a baking sheet coated with vegetable cooking spray. If room permits, add on the onions as well.

Preheat your oven broiler. Broil the eggplant on low about 6 inches from heat for 4 minutes; turn eggplant over and broil an additional 5 minutes or until lightly browned. Drizzle with the creamy dressing.

Butter the bread and sprinkle with garlic powder. Arrange eggplant, pepper, onion, herbs, tomato or whatever your favorite sandwich fixings are on the bread.

Add on the cheese and place back under the broiler open faced until the cheese is melted.

Grilled Turkey Burgers on Pita Bread
with Sweet Tomato Chutney

1 pound ground turkey
1/4 cup finely chopped onion
1 clove garlic, minced
1/2 teaspoon salt
1/8 teaspoon pepper
1/4 teaspoon dried basil
1/8 teaspoon dried thyme
1/8 teaspoon rubbed sage
2 whole pitas

Serves 4

Sweet Tomato Chutney:
1 whole head garlic, peeled and
  chopped
1 (2-inch) piece of fresh ginger,
  peeled and chopped
1 1/2 cups red wine vinegar
2 pounds fresh tomatoes, peeled
1 1/2 cups granulated sugar
1 1/2 teaspoons salt
1/2 teaspoon cayenne pepper
2 tablespoons golden raisins
2 tablespoons blanched slivered
  almonds

Makes 16 servings

Combine ingredients except for the pitas; shape into 4-inch patties. Place on grill over medium hot coals. Cook 8 minutes on each side or until done.

Serve the burgers on the pitas with the sweet tomato chutney.

Sweet Tomato Chutney:
Put the garlic, ginger, and 1/2 cup of vinegar in the food processor and process until smooth. In a large, heavy-bottomed pot, place the tomatoes and the rest of the vinegar, sugar, salt and cayenne. Bring to a boil. Add the puree from the food processor and simmer uncovered for about 2 hours, stirring occasionally.

When done, a film will cling to a spoon when dipped in. At this point add in the almonds and raisins.

Simmer, stirring another 5 minutes. Turn off heat and let cool. It should be as thick as honey. Refrigerate until ready to use.

Lobster Salad Roll

1 1/2 cups cooked lobster (about a 2-pound lobster), cut into 1/2-inch pieces
1/3 cup celery, minced
1/3 cup red bell pepper, minced and roasted
3 tablespoons green onion, chopped
1 tablespoon fresh parsley leaves, minced
3/4 cup mayonnaise
2 tablespoons fresh lemon juice
Pinch of salt and pepper
4 hot dog buns, toasted
3 tablespoons butter, melted

Serves 4

Combine all ingredients, except for the butter and hot dog buns, and mix well.

Open the buns and butter well, then toast in a 375 degree oven until lightly browned inside or about 10 minutes.

Spread the lobster salad evenly on the buns and serve.

Originally printed in the News-Leader, July 2005

Loose Meat Sandwiches

5 pounds ground beef
1 cup onion, finely chopped
1 cup beef broth
1/2 cup beer
4 ounces ketchup
1 tablespoon yellow mustard
1 tablespoon prepared horse-radish
2 teaspoons Worcestershire sauce
2 teaspoons salt
1 teaspoon Accent seasoning
1 teaspoon pepper

Makes 8 to 10 sandwiches

In a heavy pot brown meat with onion till thoroughly cooked.

Strain out the grease in a colander.

Add the remaining ingredients; simmer 40 minutes.

Serve on buns.

Originally printed in the News-Leader, May 2006

Original Texas-Style Chili

3 pounds beef, cut in small pieces,
   not ground
4 Anaheim chili pods, seared and
   peeled
1/2 cup beef fat
1 tablespoon dried oregano
1 tablespoon crushed cumin seeds
1 tablespoon salt
1 tablespoon cayenne pepper
1 tablespoon Tabasco sauce
2 garlic cloves, chopped
2 heaping tablespoons cornmeal

Serves 6

Sear beef in a little cooking oil until browned. Drop the seared beef, beef fat and chili pods in a pot and add enough water to keep the meat from burning. Bring to a boil, then lower heat, cover, and simmer about 30 minutes.

Take pot off the stove and add spices and garlic. Put back on the stove, bring to a boil again, lower heat, and simmer another hour, keeping the lid on. Stir when necessary, but remember that too much stirring will tear the meat. Add a little more water if anything seems seriously in danger of burning.

Take pot off the stove and skim off all or most of the grease. Mix in cornmeal, which thickens the chili and adds a tamale-like flavor. Simmer 30 minutes more until meat is done. Season to taste.

Originally printed in the News-Leader, October 2004

Potato Soup

1/2 pound bacon, chopped
1 stalk celery, diced
1 yellow onion, chopped
3 cloves garlic, minced
8 potatoes, peeled and cubed
5 cups chicken stock
   (or enough to cover potatoes)
3 tablespoons butter
4 cups heavy cream
1 cup parmesan cheese
1 cup cheddar cheese
2 green onions, minced for
   garnish
Salt and pepper to taste

Serves 4

In a Dutch oven or heavy stock pot, cook the bacon over medium heat until done. Remove bacon from pan, and set aside. Drain off all but 1/4 cup of the bacon grease.

In the remaining bacon grease sauté the celery and onion until onion begins to turn clear. Add the garlic, and continue cooking for 1 to 2 minutes. Add the cubed potatoes and toss to coat. Sauté for 3 to 4 minutes.

Add enough chicken stock to just cover the potatoes. Add in the heavy cream. Cover and simmer until potatoes are tender.

Add in the parmesan, cheddar cheese and butter and stir until melted. Puree some of the soup for desired thickness.

Garnish with green onion and bacon crumbles.

Originally printed in the News-Leader, October 2006

Reuben Sandwich

8 slices marbled rye bread
1 cup 1000 island dressing
  (see page 44)
16 ounces corned beef, sliced
1 1/2 cups sauerkraut
8 slices Swiss cheese, sliced
Soft butter

Makes 4 sandwiches

Butter one side of each slice of bread and turn over with the butter side facing down. Spread a little bit of the 1000 island dressing on the non-buttered side of the bread.

Place two pieces of Swiss cheese over the dressing. Put a layer of sauerkraut over the cheese. Top with a slice of corned beef. Add on a little more sauerkraut and another two slices of cheese. Top with the second slice of bread. Toast on a griddle or pan, turning to brown evenly. Serve with extra dressing on the side.

Originally printed in the News-Leader, September 2005

Sausage and Kraut Soup

2 tablespoons oil
1 medium onion, chopped
1 pound smoked sausage, sliced
4 cups chicken stock
1 cup beer
1 large potato, cubed
1 stalk celery, chopped
1 carrot, diced
2 tablespoons apple cider vinegar
2 teaspoons dried dill weed
3 tablespoons brown mustard
Salt and pepper to taste
16 ounces sauerkraut

Serves 6

Heat oil in stock pot. Sauté onions and celery until translucent.

Add in the sausage and sauté for a couple of minutes.

Add in the chicken stock and beer.

Add in the potatoes and carrots, dill weed, mustard, salt and pepper.

Cook for 1 hour or until the potatoes are tender.

Originally printed in the News-Leader, July 2005

Sour Cherry Soup

2 pounds sour cherries, pitted
4 tablespoons flour
2 cups sour cream
2 tablespoons powdered sugar
1/4 teaspoon salt
1 pinch of ground cloves
2 tablespoons lemon juice
4 cups water

Serves 6

Heat the cherries with juice in saucepan over medium heat. Whisk together the flour, sour cream, powdered sugar, salt and cloves in small bowl. Whisk in 1 cup of hot cherry mixture to temper it, then gradually whisk the sour cream mixture into the cherries in saucepan.

Stir in 4 cups of water. Cook, stirring until thickened. Use a bit more water if necessary to thin the soup to the consistency of heavy cream. Add the lemon juice. Transfer to a bowl and chill for at least 1 hour.

Strawberry Soup

2 pints fresh strawberries
1 cup orange juice
1 1/2 teaspoons quick-cooking
  tapioca
1 cup buttermilk
1/2 cup sugar
1 tablespoon lemon juice
1 teaspoon grated orange rind
1/4 teaspoon cinnamon

Serves 4

Wash and hull berries then puree.

Add in the orange juice, tapioca, and cinnamon. Pour into a casserole dish and microwave 5-6 minutes.

Stir in buttermilk, lemon juice and grated rind.

Chill, covered, until ready to serve.

Originally printed in the News-Leader, July 2005

Stuffed Burgers

1 pound ground beef
2 tablespoons blue cheese
4 tablespoons bacon crumbles
1 teaspoon garlic powder
Salt and pepper to taste

Serves 4

Add salt, pepper and garlic powder to the ground beef and mix. Hand patty the meat to form 8 individual, like-size patties.

Place 1 tablespoon of bacon crumbles in the middle of one patty and top with one-fourth of the blue cheese. Do this with three other patties. Cover each bottom patty with another burger and crimp the edges shut to seal.

Chill for one hour to set, then season with more salt and pepper and grill.

Originally printed in the News-Leader, October 2003

The Classic Hawaiian Spam Sandwich

1 can Spam, cut into 8 slices
1 can pineapple rings
4 slices American cheese
4 hamburger buns

Serves 4

Brown Spam slices in skillet. Place 2 Spam slices on each bottom half of hamburger bun. Brown the pineapple rings slightly in the same skillet. Place on top of the Spam and cover with the cheese slice. Cover sandwich with top half of bun.

Originally printed in the News-Leader, October 2005

The Classic Submarine

1/4 cup Italian vinaigrette
1 long crusty loaf French or
   Italian bread
1/4 cup mayonnaise
2 small ripe tomatoes, sliced
4 ounces prosciutto, sliced
6 ounces Italian salami, sliced
3 ounces cheddar cheese, sliced
6 ounces boiled ham, sliced
4 ounces provolone cheese, sliced
12 slices dill pickles
1 cup iceberg lettuce, shredded
12 small sweet pickled peppers,
   sliced

Serves 3 to 4

Slice a loaf of bread in half lengthwise and spread both cut sides with mayonnaise. Layer bottom half of loaf with tomato slices, prosciutto, salami, cheddar, ham, provolone and pickles.

Top with lettuce and pickled peppers.

Spoon vinaigrette over the filling and cover with top half. Press down firmly.

Originally printed in the News-Leader, March 2005

Three Cheese Italian Subs

4 ounces shredded parmesan
   cheese
4 ounces ricotta cheese, well
   drained
1 teaspoon garlic powder
6 ounces of mozzarella cheese,
   sliced
8 fresh basil leaves, minced well
2 tomatoes, sliced thin
1 teaspoon dried oregano
1/4 cup black olives, diced small
3 tablespoons extra virgin olive
   oil
Salt and pepper to taste

Serves 4

Preheat an oven to 425 degrees.
Lay the sliced tomatoes on a wax-paper-lined baking sheet.

Season the tomatoes with salt and pepper, oregano and a drizzle of olive oil. Bake in the oven for about 8 minutes then remove and cool.

Combine the parmesan cheese, drained ricotta, garlic powder, basil and olives. Season with salt and pepper and stir in about a tablespoon of the olive oil.

Slice the Italian bread loaf in half lengthwise and spread on the cheese mixture. Lay the tomatoes on top of the cheese. Place the sliced mozzarella on top of this.
Lay the top half of the bread back on top.

Place the bread on some aluminum foil and drizzle with the remaining olive oil. Wrap the bread in the foil tightly and place in the oven for about 10 to 15 minutes or until the cheese is gooey and the bread well toasted.

Vegetarian White Bean Chili

3 tablespoons olive oil
1 cup yellow onion, diced
1 cup red bell pepper, diced
1/2 cup carrots, diced
2 tablespoons minced garlic
3 cans fire-roasted chilies
32 ounces vegetable stock
3 cans cooked white cannellini
  beans
2 tablespoons ground cumin
1 tablespoon pepper sauce
Salt and pepper to taste

Serves 8

In a heavy bottom pot, sauté the onions, bell pepper and carrots until they start to soften, about 10 minutes.

Add in the garlic and chilies and cook for another two minutes.

Add in the remaining ingredients. Bring to a boil then reduce the heat and simmer for about 20 minutes.

For a thicker soup use a stick blender or potato masher to smash some of the beans.

Vidalia Onion - French Onion Soup

6 tablespoons butter
1 tablespoon olive oil
4 pounds Vidalia onions,
  peeled and thinly sliced
1 teaspoon sugar
1 tablespoon flour
6 cups beef stock
4 cups chicken stock
2 cups apple cider
2 cups dry white wine
1 baguette, cut into slices and
  toasted
1/2 pound Gruy re cheese,
  shredded
1/2 pound provolone cheese,
  sliced thin

Makes 6 to 8 servings

In a heavy pot cook the onions in the melted butter and oil, covered for about 30 minutes. Increase heat to medium-high, uncover, and add the sugar and season to taste with salt. Sauté, stirring often until onions are very soft and a deep golden brown.

Reduce heat to medium, sprinkle in flour and cook, stirring constantly for 2 to 3 minutes. Add in the wine and cook until almost reduced. Add in the remaining stock and bring to a boil then reduce the heat and simmer for about 30 minutes. Adjust the seasonings.

Ladle the soup into ovenproof bowls leaving about a half inch of clearance between the soup and the top of the bowl; top with a piece of the toasted bread. Spread the cheese on top of bread. Set bowls on a sheet tray and place under the preheated oven broiler until well browned. Remove from the oven and serve.

Originally printed in the News-Leader, March 2005

Entrées

Apple and Horseradish-Glazed Salmon

1/3 cup apple jelly
1 teaspoon chives, minced
2 tablespoons horseradish
1 tablespoon vinegar
4 (6-ounce) salmon fillets or
   steaks
1/4 teaspoon pepper
1/4 teaspoon salt
2 teaspoons olive oil

Serves 4

Combine apple jelly, chives, horseradish, vinegar and 1/4 teaspoon salt, stirring well. Season salmon with 1/4 teaspoon salt and pepper.

Heat grill to medium heat. Add salmon and grill 3 to 4 minutes. Turn salmon over; brush with half of apple mixture. Continue to grill until just medium, about 3 more minutes. Drizzle with remaining sauce.

Originally printed in the News-Leader, June 2006

Apple Glazed Pork Loaf

2 tablespoons olive oil
1/2 cup red bell pepper, chopped
1/2 cup onion, finely chopped
2 pounds lean ground pork
1/4 cup applesauce
1/4 cup ketchup
1 teaspoon hot pepper sauce
3/4 cup dry bread crumbs
1/4 cup grated parmesan cheese
2 eggs
2 tablespoons Worcestershire
   sauce
2 teaspoons dry mustard
2 teaspoons salt
1/2 teaspoon black pepper

Glaze:
1 cup apple cider
1/4 cup apple cider vinegar
1/2 cup apple sauce
1/2 cup brown sugar
1 teaspoon dry mustard
1/4 teaspoon salt

Serves 6

Sauté the bell peppers and onions in the olive oil until tender then allow to cool.

After cooling, blend together all ingredients well. Form into a loaf and place in an ungreased baking pan.

Bake at 350 degrees for about an hour. If using a thermometer, you want a temperature of 160 degrees. While the meatloaf is baking make the apple glaze below.

When the meatloaf is done, brush with the apple glaze. Place the glazed pork loaf back in the oven for about 10 minutes to warm the glaze.

Glaze:
Place all of the ingredients in a saucepan and cook over medium-high heat. Reduce to a glaze consistency, cooking for about 30 minutes.

Originally printed in the News-Leader, April 2007

Asiago Crusted Oven Baked Chicken

1 1/2 cups dry bread crumbs,
  (Panko style from the Asian
  market)
1/2 cup grated Asiago cheese
1 tablespoon ground oregano
1 teaspoon ground thyme
1/2 teaspoon pepper
1/2 teaspoon salt
1 clove garlic, minced
3/4 cup melted butter
6 bone-in chicken breasts (you
  can use boneless if desired)

Serves 6

Combine bread crumbs, cheese, oregano, thyme, pepper and salt; set aside. In a skillet add 2 tablespoons butter, sauté garlic until tender. Add remaining melted butter.

Dip chicken in garlic butter; roll each piece in bread crumb and cheese mixture.

Place chicken in a 13x9x2-inch baking pan; sprinkle with remaining bread crumb mixture and pour remaining garlic butter over all.

Bake chicken at 350 degrees for 45 minutes or until golden brown and done inside.

Asian Flank Steak

2 cloves garlic, minced
1/4 cup green onions
2 tablespoons fresh ground ginger
1/4 cup ketchup
1/4 cup pineapple juice
1/4 cup plum sauce
1/4 cup soy sauce
1/4 cup hoisin sauce
  (from the local Asian market)
1 1/2 pounds flank steak

Serves 4

Combine the garlic, ginger, onion, ketchup, pineapple juice, plum sauce, hoisin sauce and soy sauce.

Reserve about one fourth of the marinade to be used for basting as the steak cooks.

Marinate the steak for at least eight hours or overnight, which I prefer.

Broil or grill the steak using high heat, basting with the reserved marinade. This dish needs to be cooked medium to medium rare as overcooking this cut of beef can make it very tough

Cut the steak on a bias against the grain and serve with stir fried rice or some Asian noodles with stir fried vegetables.

Originally printed in the News-Leader, September 2005

Bacon Wrapped Pheasant with Orange and Sage

2 pheasant breasts, trimmed
2 fresh sage leaves, cut in half
4 slices of orange, rind removed
6 slices of bacon
1 ounce olive oil

Sauce:
1 cup orange juice
3 tablespoons red wine
1 tablespoon balsamic vinegar
1 tablespoon butter
Salt and pepper to taste

Serves 2

Butterfly open the pheasant breast. Slightly pound the breasts with a meat mallet to even out. Place a sage leaf and an orange on each breast. Lightly salt and pepper the pheasant.

Fold the breast up and wrap with three slices of bacon.

In a non-stick frying pan, fry the pheasant about 4 minutes or until the bacon starts to crisp up.

Place the bacon wrapped breasts on a baking sheet and place in a 425 degree oven for about 8 minutes or until cooked through.

Do not overcook as pheasant can become tough.

Sauce:
Heat the orange juice, red wine and balsamic vinegar in a small pan. Simmer gently for 6 to 8 minutes or until reduced by half, stirring occasionally. Stir in the butter.

Transfer the pheasant onto a serving plate, cut on the bias into pieces and drizzle the sauce over.

Originally printed in the News-Leader, November 2005

Beef Stew

1/2 pound sliced bacon, diced
6 pounds boneless shoulder
   tender, cut into 2-inch pieces
2 teaspoons salt
2 teaspoons freshly ground black
   pepper
2 cups all-purpose flour
3 cloves garlic, finely chopped
1 large onion, finely chopped
1 cup burgundy
4 cups beef stock
2 teaspoons sugar
4 cups carrots, cut into 1-inch
   pieces
2 large onions, sliced
3 pounds yellow gold
   potatoes, cut into 1/2-inch
   pieces
4 sprigs of fresh thyme
1 bay leaf
1/2 cup dry white wine
chopped parsley

Makes about 12 servings

In a large mixing bowl place the beef cubes, salt, pepper and flour. Toss to coat the meat evenly.

Use a large frying pan to sauté the bacon. Remove the bacon when crisp and reserve the fat.

In batches, brown the meat in the reserved bacon fat. If you run out of fat, use a little oil.

Transfer the browned meat to a 10-quart stove top Dutch oven, leaving about 1/4 cup of fat in the frying pan.

Add the garlic and yellow onion to the original frying pan and sauté until the onion begins to color a bit. Deglaze the frying pan with the red wine and gently scrape the bottom of the pan to get the stuck bits of food free.

Add the garlic-onion-wine mixture to the beef along with the reserved bacon pieces, beef stock and sugar. Cover and simmer for 1 1/2 hours or until tender.

Add the remaining ingredients to the pot and simmer, covered, for about 20 minutes until the vegetables are tender. Season and garnish with parsley.

Originally printed in the News-Leader, January 2006

Blackened Catfish with Kiwi Salsa

4 catfish fillets
1 teaspoon garlic powder
1 teaspoon onion powder
1 teaspoon cayenne pepper
1 teaspoon black pepper
1 teaspoon salt
1 tablespoon dried thyme leaves,
    crushed
1/2 teaspoon oregano
2 tablespoons paprika
1/2 cup peanut oil for frying
1/4 cup butter melted
Juice of one lemon

Serves 4

Kiwi Salsa:
2 kiwi, peeled and diced
1 orange, peeled and diced
1/2 cup red bell pepper, diced
2 tablespoons parsley, chopped
1 tablespoon lime juice
1 tablespoon olive oil
1 small jalapeno pepper,
    minced, seeds and veins removed
Salt and pepper to taste

Makes about 2-1/2 cups

Mix all dry ingredients together. Coat fillets evenly with mixture.

Heat small amount of oil in a heavy skillet until hot. Place fillets in skillet. Cook 3-5 minutes on each side.

Drizzle with lemon and butter.

Kiwi Salsa:
In a large bowl, combine all ingredients, mixing well. Chill briefly.

Originally printed in the News-Leader, January 2007

Braised Lamb with Orange Marinade

6-pound leg of lamb
1 tablespoon dried oregano
4 cloves garlic, minced
1 large onion, thinly sliced
2 bay leaves
3 cups orange juice
1 cinnamon stick
1 orange, cut into slices
2 cups white wine
1 teaspoon salt, or to taste
1 teaspoon ground black pepper,
   or to taste
2 tablespoons vegetable oil
3 tablespoons butter

Serves 8 - 10

Combine the orange juice with the garlic, onion, oregano, bay leaf, orange slices and white wine in a large bowl. Place meat into the marinade, cover, and refrigerate for 24 hours.

In a large pot, heat oil over medium high heat. Remove the meat from the marinade; place the meat into the pan and sear on all sides. Decrease heat to low. Pour marinade over meat in the pan and cover.

Bake in a 325 degree oven until the meat is fork tender, about 2 hours. Baste the leg as it cooks. When done remove the lamb from the pot and strain out the pan juices into another pot. Heat the pan juices on medium high until reduced by half. Add in the butter and serve over the lamb.

Originally printed in the News-Leader, April 2006

Broiled Salmon with a Horseradish Crust

4 (5 ounce) salmon fillets, skinned
   and boned
1 1/4 cups fresh bread crumbs
4 tablespoons fresh horseradish,
   grated or 1/2 cup prepared
   horseradish, squeezed dry
1 tablespoon vegetable oil
1 tablespoon rice wine
2 tablespoons mayonnaise
Salt and pepper to taste

Serves 4

Preheat the broiler. Lightly oil a baking sheet. Set salmon on the baking sheet and lightly season with salt and pepper.

In a food processor, combine bread crumbs, horseradish, oil and rice wine Process until well blended and moist.

Spread a thin layer of mayonnaise on each piece of fish. Press 1/4 of the crumb mixture over the top of the mayonnaise on each salmon fillet.

Broil on low heat about 8 inches from the heat source, until the crust is golden brown, and the salmon is opaque in the center, about 6 to 8 minutes.

Originally printed in the News-Leader, October 2006

Chef Rice's Halloween Pumpkin Curry

1 (2 pound) sugar pumpkin
1 small yellow onion, diced
1 red bell pepper, diced
1 yellow bell pepper, diced
1/2 tablespoon cumin
4 tablespoons curry powder
1/2 tablespoon red pepper flakes
1/2 cup honey
1/4 cup pistachios
1/4 cup dates, chopped
1/4 cup white raisins
2 cups heavy whipping cream
Salt and pepper to taste

Serves 6

Peel the pumpkin using a vegetable peeler. If the skin is too tough place the pumpkin in boiling water for 4 to 5 minutes then put it into ice water. The outer skin will peel off much more easily. Scoop out the stringy pulp and seeds. Reserve the seeds for roasting and eating.

Cut the remaining pumpkin flesh into bite size cubes. Boil the cubes in slightly salted water for 5 minutes to soften. Do not over boil as you will lose the firm texture that fresh pumpkin offers.

While the pumpkin cooks, heat a saut   pan and add in the cooking oil. Sautee the onion and pepper until they start to brown or caramelize. Drain the pumpkin and toss in with the pepper/onion mix. Add in the remaining ingredients and bring up to a serving temperature. Sample so you can adjust the flavors to your liking.

Since curry powders vary greatly please take these measurements as a guide only. Adjust to your own level of sweetness and spicy heat. For another twist substitute coconut milk instead of the whipping cream.

Originally printed in the News-Leader, October 2003

Chef Lou hiding out in Mexico

Chicken Cordon Bleu

4 boneless chicken breasts
4 (1-ounce) slices cooked ham
  (no water added)
1/4 cup Swiss cheese
  (like gruyere), grated
1/2 teaspoon dried thyme
2 tablespoons white wine
Salt and pepper to taste
1/4 cup flour; seasoned with salt
  and pepper
2 large eggs
1 tablespoon water
1 cup seasoned breadcrumbs
1/4 cup olive oil
5 tablespoons butter

Serves 4

Preheat oven to 400 degrees. Place each chicken breast half between sheets of plastic wrap and pound with a meat mallet to about 1/8 inch thickness.

Place a slice of cheese on each ham slice and sprinkle lightly with thyme and salt and pepper to taste. Roll up seasoned ham and cheese (jellyroll-style), then roll each chicken breast with ham and cheese inside. Tuck in ends and fasten with toothpicks.

Put seasoned flour in a bowl. Mix eggs and water in a second bowl and place bread crumbs in a third bowl. Coat breasts well with seasoned flour, roll in the egg mix, and then roll in bread crumbs.

Heat oil in frying pan. Add butter and when butter is foaming, cook chicken until all sides have developed a golden brown exterior.

Remove the chicken and place it in a preheated 400 degree oven and bake it for about 20 minutes or until chicken is golden brown and juices run clear. The internal temperature should be at least 160 degrees.

Allow the chicken to sit for 5 minutes covered then serve with lemon caper supreme sauce (see page 159).

Originally printed in the News-Leader, May 2006

Chicken with Eggplant

2 boneless skinless chicken
   breasts, cut into bite size
1-1/2 pounds eggplant, cut into
   small size wedges or French fry
   cuts. Salt and drain for an hour
   then rinse and pat dry.
4 cups oil for deep frying
2 cups of stir fry veggies like
   carrots, sliced red bell peppers,
   scallions and bamboo shoots.
2 teaspoons ginger, grated
2 teaspoons garlic, minced
1 tablespoon black bean sauce
1/4 cup chicken stock
2 teaspoons sugar
2 tablespoons oyster sauce
2 teaspoons soy sauce to taste

Serves 4

Marinate the chicken in a little soy sauce, oil, garlic and rice wine vinegar for an hour.

Cut eggplant into small size wedges or French fry cuts. Salt and drain for an hour then rinse and pat dry. (I prefer to leave the skin on).

This is a simple stir fry dish with one twist. Heat the peanut oil to 350 degrees. Deep fry the eggplant pieces for about 2 minutes then drain them.

Then like a regular stir fry, start with the chicken followed by the veggies, the spices, sauces and stock then finish up with the eggplant.

Originally printed in the News-Leader, January 2004

Chili Relleno-Grilled

4 large poblano chilies
2 tablespoons olive oil
1 medium onion, finely chopped
2 cloves garlic, finely chopped
2 jalapenos, seeded and chopped
   (leave seeds in for spicier filling)
1/2 red bell pepper, finely
   chopped
1 tablespoon ground cumin
2 (16 ounce) cans black beans,
   drained
3 teaspoons hot sauce
3 cups Pepper Jack cheese,
   coarsely grated
Salt and pepper to taste

Serves 4

Cut poblano chilies in half lengthwise to create a boat for filling and scrape out seeds.

Heat 2 tablespoons olive oil in a nonstick skillet. Add onion, garlic, jalapenos, red bell pepper and cumin. Cook over medium heat until golden brown, about 4 minutes.

Remove pan from heat and stir in black beans, hot sauce and 2 cups of the cheese. Add salt and pepper to taste. Spoon the mixture into the hollowed chilies and sprinkle with remaining cheese.

Set up grill for indirect grilling and preheat to medium. Arrange the chilies on the grill away from the heat. Cook until chilies are tender and cheese is browned and bubbling, 30 to 40 minutes.

Originally printed in the News-Leader, July 2004

Classic Beef Wellington

4 (5 ounce) beef fillets, trimmed
2 tablespoons butter
2 tablespoons olive oil
4 tablespoons onion, minced
8 ounces mushrooms,
   chopped fine
1 cup Madeira wine
4 tablespoons heavy cream
Salt and pepper to taste
2 pounds puff pastry

Wine Sauce:
1 tablespoon olive oil
4 tablespoons onions, minced
1 cup Madeira wine
1 cup beef stock
8 tablespoons butter
1/2 teaspoon black pepper
1 teaspoon dried thyme
1 teaspoon honey

Serves 4

Salt and pepper the beef fillets and over high heat in a pan, sauté filets mignons in butter for 30 seconds on each side. Set aside to cool.

Reduce the pan heat to medium and add in the olive oil, onions and mushrooms and cook until all liquid is evaporated. Add wine and reduce completely. Add cream and reduce to a thick puree. Check the seasonings.

Preheat oven to 400 degrees. Divide the puff pastry into 4 6x12-inch portions, approximately 1/4-inch thick.

Place a spoonful of the mushroom mixture in the center of each pastry.

Place a filet on top of the mushroom mixture.

Brush the pastry edges with egg wash (egg and water) and fold it over. Shape edges of pastry to contours of meat.

Turn the pastry over and glaze the top of pastry with more egg wash.

Bake for 20 minutes or until golden brown.

Wine Sauce:
In a sauté pan over medium heat, add olive oil, onions, pepper and thyme. Sauté until onions are soft.

Add in the Madeira wine and honey and reduce by half.

Add beef stock and reduce by half again.

Whisk in the butter and season with salt to taste. Keep warm.

Originally printed in the News-Leader, August 2005

Coq AU Vin

1 whole stewing chicken
Kosher salt and black pepper
1/4 to 1/2 cup all-purpose flour
2 tablespoons water
6 slices bacon
8 ounces button mushrooms
1 tablespoon unsalted butter
1 cup red wine
2 tablespoons tomato paste
1 medium onion, quartered
2 stalks celery, quartered
2 medium carrots, quartered
3 cloves garlic, crushed
6 to 8 sprigs fresh thyme
1 bay leaf
2 cups chicken stock or broth

Serves 4

Cut chicken into 8 serving pieces. Sprinkle the chicken on all sides with kosher salt and freshly ground black pepper. Place the chicken pieces, into a large (1- or 2- gallon) sealable plastic bag along with the flour. Shake to coat all of the pieces of the chicken. Remove the chicken from the bag to a metal rack. Cook bacon in a large Dutch oven until crisp then remove.

In the same pan, add in the onions, sprinkle with salt and pepper, and saute until golden, approximately 8 to 10 minutes. Remove the onions from the pan and set aside.

Next, brown the chicken pieces on each side until golden brown, working in batches if necessary to not overcrowd the pan. Quarter the mushrooms and add. Follow with the remaining ingredients. Bake in a preheated 325 degree oven for 1-1/2 to 2 hours.

Crab Stuffed Shrimp with Bacon Wrapper

24 (16-20 count per pound)
   shrimp, tail on
1 tablespoon olive oil
3 tablespoons minced onion
2 tablespoons minced celery
2 tablespoons minced red bell
   pepper
2 tablespoons mayonnaise
2 teaspoons Old Bay seasoning
1 teaspoon garlic powder
1 tablespoon lemon juice
Salt and pepper to taste
1 pound real crab meat
   (claw meat is fine)
12 slices of bacon

Serves 4

In a hot sauté pan, cook the onion, celery and bell pepper until tender. When tender mix with the crab meat in a bowl.

Stir in the mayonnaise, lemon and seasonings and set aside.

In a sauté pan lay out the bacon and cook until it is just starting to crisp, then remove from the heat and set on a paper towel.

Using a paring knife split the back of the shrimp about three fourths of the way through from one end to the other. Clean the shrimp out if needed.

Into the cut stuff some of the crab mixture.Cut a slice of bacon in half and wrap it around the stuffed shrimp. Use a toothpick to hold the bacon to the shrimp.

Bake the shrimp in a preheated 350 degree oven for about 10 minutes, then turn the shrimp over and cook for another 10 minutes.

Deep Dish Stuffed Pizza

1 envelope yeast
1 3/4 cups lukewarm water
1/2 cup vegetable oil
1/4 cup olive oil
1/2 cup cornmeal
5 cups all-purpose flour
1 tablespoon salt
1 pound mozzarella cheese,
   shredded
2 cups Italian sausage, cooked
   and crumbled
1 cup mushrooms, sliced
3 cups canned plum tomatoes,
   drained and chopped
1 teaspoon dried basil
1 teaspoon dried oregano
2 cloves garlic, crushed
3 tablespoons olive oil
Salt to taste
4 tablespoons parmesan cheese

Makes 2 pizzas and
   serves 8 to 10

Place the water in a mixing bowl of a stand mixer. Sprinkle the yeast over the water, and let stand for 5 minutes to dissolve. Pour in the vegetable oil, olive oil, cornmeal, salt and 3 cups of the flour. Mix with the beater for 10 minutes. Add the remaining flour, and switch from the beater to the dough hook. Mix for about 5 minutes. The dough will be pretty moist.

Pour the dough out onto a floured surface and cover with a large bowl. Allow to rise until doubled in bulk, about 1 hour. Punch down the dough and let rise again.

For the topping combine the tomatoes, basil, oregano, garlic, salt and olive oil and set aside.

Preheat the oven to 475 degrees. Grease two 9- or 10-inch round cake pans or spring form pans.

Divide the dough evenly between the two pans. Press the dough out so that it goes all the way up the sides of the pans.

Place the mozzarella cheese into the crusts, layering the mushrooms and sausage in with the cheese.

Bake for 35 to 40 minutes in the preheated oven until the top is golden and gooey and the crust a light golden brown.

Add on the tomatoes and bake for an additional 5 minutes just to warm the top. Sprinkle with grated parmesan and you're ready to go.

Originally printed in the News-Leader, March 2007

Grilled Tomato Soup with Parmesan Cheese Dumplings

4 ripe tomatoes, halved and
   seeded
1/2 red bell pepper, diced large and
   seeded
1/4 cup carrot, thinly sliced
6 tablespoons olive oil
2 cloves garlic, sliced
1/2 small yellow onion, sliced
6 cups chicken stock
1 cup whipping cream
1/2 teaspoon liquid smoke
1 teaspoon salt
1 teaspoon freshly ground black
   pepper
Dash of chipotle Tabasco sauce

Parmesan Cheese Dumplings:
2 ounces cream cheese
2 ounces heavy whipping cream
1 egg white, whipped
2 egg yolks
3/4 cup parmesan cheese, grated
1/2 cup flour
2 tablespoons chives, minced
1/2 teaspoon salt
Pinch of garlic powder

Serves 4

Preheat the grill pan until extremely hot. Toss the onions, carrots and peppers with 3 tablespoons olive oil and then add them to the grill pan and grill for 4 to 5 minutes.

Add in the garlic and cook for one more minute turning the vegetables over as they grill. Add the grilled vegetables to the stock pot and fill with the chicken stock.

Place the seeded tomatoes in a large bowl and toss with 3 tablespoons of the olive oil. Set the tomatoes cut-side down on the grill and grill for about 3 minutes, turning over halfway through the cooking time.

Add the tomato to the stock pot and simmer for 20 minutes or until tender. Pass the soup through a food mill and then strain into a saucepan using a china cap strainer.

Add in the cream, liquid smoke, Tabasco and salt and pepper.

Parmesan Cheese Dumplings:
In a mixing bowl mix the cream cheese and all of the eggs' yolks with a wooden spoon, until incorporated. Add in the parmesan cheese, spices chives, and flour. Mix until the dough comes together. Fold in the egg whites. Cover and refrigerate for 10 minutes.

With two spoons, scoop out 2 tablespoons of dough and form into a dumpling shape. Drop the dough into boiling water and cook until the dumplings float.

Place two dumplings in each bowl of soup.

Originally printed in the News-Leader, March 2005

Hoisin Glazed Pork Chops

3 tablespoons hoisin sauce
4 teaspoons brown sugar
4 teaspoons green onion, minced
1 1/2 teaspoons lemon juice
1 1/2 teaspoons soy sauce
3 boneless pork loin chops, cut
   1-inch thick

Serves 3

Combine the hoisin sauce, brown sugar, green onion, lemon juice and soy sauce in a bowl. Remove half of the marinade for basting later. Add the pork chops to the bowl and allow to marinate for about 2 hours or longer.

Preheat the oven broiler to low.

Remove the chops from the marinade and place on a rack in a broiler pan.

Broil about 8 inches from the broiler for 5 minutes then turn once and broil for another 4 to 5 minutes.

Use the reserved marinade for a basting sauce as the meat cooks.

Originally printed in the News-Leader, April 2005

Honey Roast Duck with Port and Orange Sauce

1 whole duck
Salt and pepper
2 tablespoons honey
1/4 cup chicken stock

Sauce:
1 ounce flour
2 tablespoons duck fat from
   roasting pan
2 ounces Port wine
The juice and grated rind from
   one orange
1 tablespoon red currant jelly
Salt and pepper to taste
2 cups chicken stock

Serves 4

Preheat oven to 325 degrees.
Sprinkle the duck with salt and pepper inside and out. Put the duck in a roasting pan on top of a rack to keep it out of its own fat and roast for 1-1/2 hours.

Mix the honey with the 1/4-cup measure of chicken stock. Remove the duck from the oven and drain off the grease. Prick the duck skin with a fork and brush in the honey mixture. Return the duck to the oven and cook for a further 30 minutes.

Take 2 tablespoons of the poured off duck fat and add in the flour; cook for one minute.

Add the rest of the sauce ingredients and bring to a boil, stirring continuously. Reduce heat and simmer gently until the sauce is of a smooth consistency.

Serve the sauce hot with the roast duck.

Originally printed in the News-Leader, November 2005

Mexicali Pork Roast

2 tablespoons vegetable oil
1/2 cup red bell pepper, diced
1/2 cup green bell pepper, diced
1/2 cup onion, diced
2 cloves of garlic, smashed
1 1/4 pound ground pork
1/4 pound chorizo sausage
2 large eggs
2 teaspoons salt
1 teaspoon pepper
2 tablespoons jalapeno hot sauce
1/2 cup dry bread crumbs
1/2 cup salsa, store bought
1/4 cup finely ground tortilla chips

Topping:
2 cups salsa of your choice
1 cup cheddar cheese, grated

Serves 4

Sauté the onions, peppers and garlic in the vegetable oil until tender and allow them to cool.

When the vegetables are cool combine them with all of the remaining ingredients and mix well.

Form the meat into a loaf and bake in a 350 degree oven for about an hour.

When the temperature is 160 degrees, remove the pork loaf from the oven and top with the salsa and then the cheese.

Place back into the oven until the cheese is melted.

Originally printed in the News-Leader, April 2007

Mock London Broil

Marinade:
1/2 teaspoon kosher salt
1 teaspoon ground black pepper
1/4 teaspoon dried thyme
1 large clove garlic, minced
1/2 onion, diced
1 bay leaf
1 cup stout or dark ale
1/2 cup vegetable oil
1 tablespoon honey
2 tablespoons red wine vinegar
1 tablespoon Worcestershire
   sauce
2 pounds ribeye steak or chuck
   tender steaks cut at least 1 inch
   thick

Makes 4 to 5 servings

Combine the marinade ingredients, pour into a zip lock bag and add in the meat.

Let sit overnight.

Preheat grill.

Grill the beef for about 5 minutes on each side then cut against the grain in very thin slices.

Originally printed in the News-Leader, January 2006

Old Fashioned Pork Roast in a Cast Iron Dutch Oven

4-5 pounds of pork butt or
 shoulder
5 cloves garlic, peeled
1 onion, thinly sliced
2 tablespoons horseradish
2 bay leaves
2 cups chicken stock
1 tablespoon Kitchen Bouquet
2 teaspoons black pepper
1 teaspoon salt
1 tablespoon lard or vegetable oil
2 tablespoons cornstarch
1/2 cup water

Serves 6

Preheat oven to 350 degrees. Melt lard in cast iron Dutch oven over medium high heat. Salt and pepper all sides of pork roast. When lard is hot, place roast in the Dutch oven. Brown the roast on all sides in the fat.

Lay garlic cloves and onion slices around the roast and stir to brown them a bit.

Mix Kitchen Bouquet into the 2 cups of chicken stock with the horseradish. Pour this over the pork and bring to a boil. Reduce the heat and cover tightly. Place in lower portion of the oven. Roast 1 hour for boneless roast; 1-3/4 hours for bone-in roast.

Halfway through roasting time turn the roast over. When done, remove the roast from pan and cover to keep hot. Mix 2 tablespoons cornstarch into 1/2 cup water. Using a whisk, stir the cornstarch mixture into the pot drippings, breaking up the garlic cloves as you mix. Bring to a boil to thicken, then serve.

Originally printed in the News-Leader, October 2005

Old Fashioned Turkey and Black Bean Enchiladas

1/2 cup vegetable oil
12 (6-inch) corn tortillas
3 cups cooked turkey
10 ounces sharp cheddar, grated
 (about 3 cups)
1 (14-ounce) can of seasoned black
 beans
2 tablespoons lime juice
1 tablespoon ground cumin
1 cup chopped red onion
2 cups enchilada sauce
2 ripe avocados
4 tablespoons sour cream

Serve 4 to 6

In a skillet heat the oil over moderately high heat until it is hot but not smoking. Cook the tortillas one at a time for 5 seconds or until they are softened but not crisp. Let drain on paper towels.

On each tortilla mound 1/4-cup of the turkey, 1 table-spoon of the cheddar, 1 tablespoon of the onion, 3 table-spoons of black beans and a splash of lime juice. Roll up the tortillas jelly-roll fashion, and arrange the enchiladas, seam side down, in a shallow baking dish.

Pour the sauce over the enchiladas and sprinkle with the remaining cheddar. Bake them in a 350 degree oven for 15 to 20 minutes until the cheese is bubbly. Garnish the enchiladas with diced avocado and a dollop of sour cream.

Originally printed in the News-Leader, November 2003

Osso Buco

4 (2-inch-thick) veal shanks, tied
  securely with kitchen string
  to keep the meat attached to the
  bone
All-purpose flour for dredging the
  veal shanks
4 tablespoons unsalted butter
  plus additional if necessary
3 tablespoons olive oil plus
  additional if necessary
1 cup dry white wine
1 cup onion, finely chopped
1/2 cup carrot, finely chopped
1/2 cup celery, finely chopped
1 tablespoon garlic, minced
6 cups beef broth or more as
  needed
2 cups tomato, peeled, seeded
  and chopped
1 teaspoon dried thyme
2 bay leaves
1 teaspoon salt
1 teaspoon pepper

Gremolata:
1 cup fresh parsley leaves,
  minced
4 tablespoons freshly grated
  lemon zest
2 tablespoons garlic, minced

Serves 4

Season the veal shanks with salt and pepper and dredge them in the flour, shaking off the excess. In a heavy skillet heat oil and butter over moderately high heat until the foam subsides. In the fat brown the veal shanks in batches, adding some of the additional butter and oil as necessary and transferring the shanks as they are browned to a platter.

Cook the onion, the carrots, the celery and the garlic in the remaining pan drippings over moderately low heat, stirring occasionally, until the vegetables are softened

Deglaze the pan with the white wine and reduce by half. Add the shanks with any juices that have accumulated. Add enough of the broth to almost cover the shanks. Spread the tomatoes over the shanks, add the spices, herbs and salt and pepper. Bring the liquid to a simmer over moderately high heat. Braise the mixture, covered, in the middle of a preheated 300 degree oven for 4 hours or until the veal is tender. Transfer the shanks with a slotted spoon to an ovenproof serving dish, discard the strings, and keep the shanks warm.

Strain the pan juices into a saucepan, pressing hard on the solids, and skim the fat. Use as a simple sauce for the veal.

Gremolata:
In a bowl stir together the parsley, the zest, and the garlic. Sprinkle the veal shanks with the gremolata and pour some of the juices around them.

Panang Curry Shrimp

1 tablespoon vegetable oil
3 garlic cloves, finely minced
1 tablespoon coconut milk
  (unsweetened)
1/4 cup minced onion
3 tablespoons panang curry paste
1 tablespoon sugar
1 teaspoon paprika
2 teaspoons salt
1 1/2 cups coconut milk (unsweetened)
1/2 tablespoon basil leaves, minced
1 cup broccoli florets
1/2 cup red bell pepper, diced
1/4 cup carrot, grated
1/2 teaspoon red pepper flakes
8 large shrimp, peeled and deveined

Serves 2

Place oil, garlic, onion, 1 tablespoon of the coconut milk, 1/2 teaspoon red pepper flakes (or more if you like it hot) and 1 tablespoon of the panang curry paste in a pan or wok and sauté until light brown, about 4 minutes.

Add sugar, paprika, remaining curry paste, salt, and coconut milk.

Bring to a boil. Add broccoli, carrot and shrimp then simmer for two minutes. Stir in basil. Serve with long grain white or brown rice.

Originally printed in the News-Leader, March 2006

Pan Seared Breast of Chicken
with an Apple Cider Brandy Glaze

4 boneless chicken breasts
Salt and pepper
1 cup apple cider glaze
1 tablespoon butter
1 tablespoon olive oil
1 tablespoon butter for sauce

Apple Cider Glaze:
2 tablespoons butter
1/4 cup diced onion
2 cloves garlic, smashed
1/2 cup brandy
1 quart apple juice
1 cup apple jelly

Serves 4

Preheat oven to 400 degrees. Season chicken liberally on each side with salt and pepper. In an ovenproof sauté pan, heat the butter and oil over high heat until hot. Sear the chicken breasts for about 3 minutes on each side or until golden brown.

Transfer the skillet to the oven and cook the chicken for about 10 to 12 minutes or until juices run clear. Remove the pan from the oven, transfer chicken to a plate and keep warm.

Place the chicken-cooking pan over high heat and deglaze the pan with the apple cider glaze. Add additional 1 tablespoon of butter to the deglazed pan. Add in the chicken breast and turn to glaze on all sides. Plate chicken and drizzle with remaining pan juice

Apple Cider Glaze:
Sweat onions in melted butter. Deglaze with brandy (AWAY FROM FLAME). Add in jelly and apple juice. Simmer for 30 minutes. Strain and store for use.

Parmesan Crusted Oven Baked Chicken

1 1/2 cups dry bread crumbs,
  (Panko style if you can find
  them)
1/2 cup grated parmesan cheese
1 tablespoon ground oregano
1 teaspoon ground thyme
1/2 teaspoon pepper
1/2 teaspoon salt
1 clove garlic, minced
3/4 cup melted butter
6 bone-in chicken breasts
  (you can use boneless if desired)

Serves 6

Combine bread crumbs, parmesan cheese, oregano, thyme, pepper, and salt; set aside. In a skillet sauté garlic in 2 tablespoons butter until tender. Add remaining butter.

Dip chicken in garlic butter; roll each piece in bread crumbs and parmesan mixture.

Place parmesan chicken in a 13x9x2-inch baking pan; sprinkle remaining bread crumb mixture and pour remaining garlic butter over all.

Bake parmesan chicken at 350 degrees for 45 minutes or until golden brown and done inside.

Originally printed in the News-Leader, October 2006

Pecan Crusted Trout

4 (4-ounce) trout fillets with
  skin on
1/4 cup flour
1 beaten egg
1 cup ground pecans
3 tablespoons vegetable oil
Lemon wedges for serving
Salt and pepper to taste

Makes 4 servings

Preheat the oven to 375 degrees. Season the fish on both sides. Dredge the fish fillets in flour, then in the beaten egg and coat them well with the pecans on the side with no skin.

Heat the oil in a large skillet over medium heat. When the oil is hot, add the fillets, nut side down. Sauté for 2 minutes, then turn the fish over and cook for another 2 minutes. Transfer the fillets to a baking sheet and bake for 10 minutes. Serve with lemon wedges.

Originally printed in the News-Leader, June 2007

Shrimp and Vegetable Tempura

2 cups all-purpose flour
2 cups club soda
1 tablespoon baking powder
2 egg yolks
8 large shrimp
1 large zucchini, sliced thick
1 large squash, sliced thick
1 head broccoli, sliced thick
1 bunch asparagus, trimmed
2 whole carrots, thinly sliced
1 whole onion, cut into strips
Peanut oil for frying
Plain or tempura flour for coating

Serves 4

Peel and devein the shrimp, leaving the tails intact. Heat the oil in a deep pan or wok to moderately hot. Cut 4 incisions in the under-section of each shrimp and straighten them out.

Coat the shrimp lightly with flour, leaving the tail uncoated, and shake off the excess.

In a bowl, gently mix the flour, baking powder, club soda and egg yolks. The batter will be lumpy, but don't over mix as this would toughen the batter. Let the batter rest for about 20 minutes.

Working with a few at a time, dip each shrimp into the batter, still leaving the tail uncoated. Fry briefly in the hot oil until lightly golden; remove from the pan and drain well on paper towels. Repeat the frying process with the vegetable pieces, doing about 2 to 3 pieces at a time.

Serve immediately with soy sauce.

Shrimp Curry

1 small onion, sliced thin
1 small red bell pepper, sliced thin
1 small carrot, shredded
2 tablespoons olive oil
1 tablespoon curry paste
1 pound peeled and deveined shrimp
1 tablespoon honey
2 cups evaporated milk
1 green onion minced
Red pepper flakes to taste
Salt and pepper to taste

Serves 4

Sauté the onion, carrot and pepper in the hot oil for about three minutes.

Add the curry paste and cook the mixture, whisking, for 1 minute.

Add the shrimp and sauté the mixture over moderately high heat, stirring, for 1 to 2 minutes or until the shrimp turn pink.

Add the evaporated milk and honey, then simmer the mixture uncovered, stirring occasionally, for 1 minute or until the shrimp are just cooked through.

Sprinkle the dish with the green onion and serve with the rice.

Originally printed in the News-Leader, June 2007

Shrimp Egg Foo Yung with Brown Sauce

Brown Sauce:
1 cup chicken broth
1 tablespoon oyster sauce
1 tablespoon soy sauce
Salt and pepper to taste
1 tablespoon cornstarch dissolved
*   in 4 tablespoons water*

Egg Foo Yung:
3/4 pound fresh shrimp, shelled
*   and deveined*
1/2 cup bean sprouts
1 medium yellow onion, sliced
*   thin*
1 red bell pepper, sliced thin
1/2 cup fresh mushrooms, sliced
*   thin*
1/2 cup water chestnuts, sliced
2 green onions, minced
Peanut oil for frying
6 large eggs
Salt and pepper, to taste
1 tablespoon Chinese rice wine or
*   dry sherry*

Serves 4

For the sauce, bring the chicken broth to a boil. Stir in the seasonings, and thicken with the cornstarch and water mixture. Keep warm and set aside.

Finely chop the shrimp. Heat 2 tablespoons of peanut oil in a frying pan. When the oil is hot, add the shrimp. Stir-fry until they turn pink and are cooked. Remove from the pan.

Next, sauté the vegetables for about 2 minutes. In a large bowl, lightly beat the eggs with the salt and pepper or soy. Stir in the rice wine or sherry, cooked shrimp and the vegetables.

In a wok or heavy bottomed pan, heat 2-1/2 inches oil for deep-frying to approximately 375 degrees. When the oil is hot, gently ladle one-fourth of the egg mixture into the wok.

Deep fry on one side until browned (about 2 minutes), then ladle a bit of oil over the top so that it firms up. Use a spatula to gently turn the egg over and brown the other side. Remove the omelet with a slotted spoon and drain on paper towels. Serve with the sauce poured over top.

Originally printed in the News-Leader, January 2007

South American Glazed Roast Pork

1 (4 1/2-5-pound) loin of pork
1 teaspoon salt
Black pepper to taste
1 cup orange juice
2 tablespoons lime juice
1/2 cup brown sugar
1 tablespoon ginger
1/2 teaspoon powdered cloves

Serves 6

Preheat the over to 325 degrees.
Season the pork with salt and pepper. Place pork, fat side up, in a roasting pan and roast for approximately an hour or until an internal temperature is 170 degrees.

While heating pork, mix the following together in a small saucepan: orange juice, lime juice, sugar, ginger, and cloves. Simmer for 30 minutes. Brush glaze over pork two times during the last 1/2 hour of roasting time.

Originally printed in the News-Leader, January 2007

Tandoori Chicken

4 chicken leg quarters, skin
  removed
2 tablespoons vegetable oil
1/2 cup onion, chopped
2 tablespoons garlic, chopped
2 tablespoons ginger, chopped
1 tablespoon paprika
2 teaspoons jalapeno pepper,
  finely chopped, seeds removed
1 1/2 teaspoons salt
1 teaspoon ground cumin
1 teaspoon turmeric
1 teaspoon ground coriander
1 teaspoon garam masala
1/2 teaspoon cayenne
1 carton plain yogurt
1 tablespoon lime juice
4 tablespoons butter, melted
Sliced limes for garnish

Serves 4

Cut diagonal slits into the chicken about 1-inch apart, and 1/2-inch deep. This allows the marinade to get into the chicken. Set the chicken aside.

In a blender, combine the oil, onion, garlic, ginger and pepper, and process on high speed to a paste. Add the paprika, salt, cumin, turmeric, coriander, garam masala and cayenne, and process until well blended. Add the yogurt and lime juice, and puree until smooth.

Pour the marinade over the chicken. Turn to coat evenly, rubbing the marinade into the slits. Cover tightly with plastic wrap and refrigerate overnight.

When ready, preheat oven to 425 degrees. Place the chicken on a wire rack over a deep pan. Spread any of the remaining marinade on the chicken.

Drizzle the melted butter over the chicken then place in the oven and bake for 35 minutes.

Originally printed in the News-Leader, January 2006

The Perfect Roast Chicken

1 (4-pound) roasting chicken
1 tablespoon fresh thyme leaves,
  minced
1 tablespoon fresh oregano,
  minced
2 teaspoons fresh parsley, minced
1/4 pound butter, softened
Salt and black pepper
2 cloves garlic, smashed
1 orange
1 onion, halved
1 onion, diced
2 carrots diced
1 rib celery diced
6 strips bacon
2 tablespoons flour
1 1/2 cups chicken broth
1/4 cup dry sherry

Serve 2 to 4

Preheat oven to 425 degrees.

Rinse the chicken with water, inside and out, and dry with paper towels. In a bowl, mash the butter with the chopped herbs. Rub the herbed butter under the skin, as well as all over the outside of the chicken. Season the bird with salt and pepper. Stuff the cavity with the orange, garlic and remaining onion.

Tie the legs together with kitchen twine and then wrap around the wings to help the bird hold its shape.

In a roasting pan, toss in the remaining diced vegetables. Place a wire rack over the vegetables and place the chicken on top breast-side up.

Lay the strips of bacon across the breast of the chicken and roast for 25 minutes. Remove the bacon and roast for another 25 minutes until the skin is brown.

An instant-read thermometer should read 165 degrees when the chicken is done. Stick the thermometer into the thickest part of the thigh for proper temperature. Other signs the chicken is done is that the juices will run clear from the bird and the joints of the leg and wing will become loose.

Remove the chicken to a platter, cover with foil and let stand for 10 minutes so the juices settle back into the meat before carving.

Next remove the vegetables from the roasting pan. Skim off as much fat as possible from the pan and leave the drippings. Place the roasting pan on top of the stove over medium heat and take a wooden spoon or spatula to scrape up the browned bits from the bottom of the pan. Stir the flour into the drippings to make a roux. Pour in the chicken broth in stages; continue to stir to dissolve the flour evenly to prevent lumps. Stir in the sherry and bring the liquid to a boil. Season with salt and pepper.

Originally printed in the News-Leader, April 2006

Side Dishes

Asparagus au Gratin

2 tablespoons butter
1 teaspoon salt
2 tablespoons flour
2 cups milk
1 cup mild cheddar cheese, grated
1/4 cup parmesan cheese, grated
1 1/2 cups Ritz cracker crumbs
1 cup walnuts, toasted
2 cups fresh asparagus spears,
    blanched and trimmed
1/2 cup cracker crumbs for the top
2 tablespoons butter

Serves 4

In a saucepan over medium-low heat, melt the butter then stir in salt and flour. Cook and stir for about 4 minutes.

Slowly stir in the milk. Add in the grated cheese in two helpings, stirring well in between each. Cook until the cheese melts and sauce is thickened, then remove from the heat.

Combine cracker crumbs with the walnuts.

In a buttered casserole, place a layer of asparagus, a layer of cracker mixture and then a layer of sauce. Repeat the layers, ending with the crumbs. Dot the top with butter.

Bake at 350 degrees for 25 minutes, or until top is browned.

Originally printed in the News-Leader, May 2005

Baked Stuffed Onions with Spinach and Cheese

2 large, sweet Vidalia onions
2 teaspoons olive oil
1 clove garlic
1 (10-ounce) package frozen
    chopped spinach, thawed and
    squeezed dry
4 slices of bacon
1 teaspoon lemon juice
1/4 cup bread crumbs
1/2 cup heavy cream
1/4 cup parmesan cheese
1/4 cup crumbled feta cheese
Salt and pepper to taste

Serves 4

Place the onions in a large pan and cover with lightly salted water. Bring to a boil and cook until the onions are partially tender, about 10 to 15 minutes. Drain and cool, then cut the onions in half crosswise. Scoop out the center of each onion half, leaving a 1/2-inch shell. Set the centers aside for later.

Prepare a shallow baking dish large enough to hold the onion halves in one layer with nonstick pan spray. Place the onions in the dish, hollowed sides up. Preheat the oven to 350 degrees. Chop the reserved centers of the onions.

Sauté the bacon until crisp then remove. Cook the reserved onion with the garlic in the bacon fat. Stir in the spinach and the lemon juice and cook until the liquid evaporates.

Remove from the heat and stir in the cream, bread crumbs, cheese and reserved chopped bacon. Fill the onion shells with the spinach mixture. Cover with plastic wrap, then foil and bake about 20 minutes. Remove the foil and bake for 10 more minutes to brown.

Originally printed in the News-Leader, April 2005

Baked Sweet Potato Fries

3 large sweet potatoes, cleaned
   with skin on
2 tablespoons olive oil
1 teaspoon salt
1/2 teaspoon black pepper
1 teaspoon garlic powder

Serves 4

Slice potatoes into 1/4-inch slices. Go back and cut again into friendly fry-size sticks.

Season with the spices and drizzle with the olive oil. Bake at 350 degrees until crisp, about 20 minutes.

Best Baked Beans

3 cans of your favorite canned
   baked beans or pork and beans
12 slices bacon
3 cups onion, minced
4 cloves garlic, minced
1 cup brown sugar
1/2 cup molasses
1 cup ketchup
2 tablespoons dry mustard
Salt and pepper to taste

Serves 6

Cook bacon until crisp. Remove and set aside.

Sauté onion in bacon grease until the onion starts to brown or caramelize. Add in garlic, brown sugar, molasses, ketchup, dry mustard and reserved crumbled bacon.

Bake, covered, at 300 degrees for 3 hours, then uncovered for 1 hour.

Originally printed in the News-Leader, June 2005

Cheesy Mashed Potatoes with Horseradish

2 pounds russet or Idaho
  potatoes, diced large
3 tablespoons butter
1 cup sharp cheddar cheese,
  shredded
1 cup Monterey Jack cheese,
  shredded
1/3 cup milk
6 tablespoons prepared
  horseradish
1 tablespoon chives, minced
4 slices of cooked bacon,
  crumbled
Salt and pepper to taste

Makes 6 servings

Cook potatoes in large pot of boiling water until very tender, about 16 minutes. Drain in a colander.

Return the potatoes to pot and mash with potato masher. Stir in butter and cheeses and mix until smooth.

Add milk to make a creamy consistency.

Stir in horseradish and half of the chives. Season to taste with salt and pepper.

Place in serving bowl and sprinkle with remaining chives and bacon.

Originally printed in the News-Leader, October 2006

Chef Lou's Sausage, Apple, Raisin Stuffing

1 loaf Texas toast - staled for one
  day, crusts removed and torn
  into chunks
1 pound roll sausage, sage
  flavored
1 large onion, diced
1 cup celery, diced
3 cloves garlic, minced
3 tablespoons butter
3 Granny Smith apples, peeled
  and diced
1 cup white raisins
6 cups chicken stock
1 1/2 tablespoons poultry
  seasoning
1 teaspoon sage
3 eggs, beaten
Salt and pepper to taste
Pan release spray

Makes 6 servings

In a heavy pot brown the sausage, then let it drain on paper towels.

Sauté the onions and celery in the remaining sausage fat until they soften and start to caramelize. Add in the minced garlic, butter, apples and raisins and cook for about 5 minutes.

Toss in the bread cubes, poultry seasoning, eggs and chicken stock. The mix should be wet enough that all of the bread is able to soak up liquid without having excess liquid left over. Add additional stock if needed. Season with salt, pepper and more poultry seasoning if needed.

Let sit for about 20 minutes so the bread absorbs the liquid. Spray a 13x9-inch baking pan with pan release spray and pour in the dressing. Bake in a preheated 365 degree oven for an hour or until firm in the middle. As with any cake you can insert a knife to see if it comes out clean.

Originally printed in the News-Leader, November 2005

Creamed Peas and Portabella

1 tablespoon butter
1 small yellow onion, diced
2 portabella mushrooms, thinly
   sliced
2 tablespoons butter
1 pound fresh or frozen peas
1 cup heavy cream
1/4 cup parmesan cheese
Salt and pepper to taste

Serves 6

Sauté the onion in 1 tablespoon of butter until tender and slightly caramelized.

Toss in the mushrooms and the additional butter. Cook until the mushrooms are tender and the liquid in the pan has cooked off.

Add in the cream and parmesan cheese and heat to serving temperature. Add in the peas, remove from heat and season.

Foil Grilled Taters and Onions

3 medium russet potatoes,
   scrubbed and thinly sliced
1 large onion, peeled and sliced
Garlic powder to taste
Paprika to taste
Salt and pepper to taste
2 tablespoons butter
2 tablespoons olive oil
Cooking spray like Pam

Serves 4

Prepare large squares of heavy duty aluminum foil with cooking spray. Place a layer of potatoes and then sprinkle with seasonings and some butter. Put a layer of onions on top of potatoes, then another layer of potatoes on onions.

Season again and add more butter. Drizzle with the olive oil. Wrap with foil, sealing edges and rolling toward center. Cook on hot grill, turning once, for 10 to 15 minutes. These may also be cooked in a 400 degree oven for the same length of time.

Originally printed in the News-Leader, August 2006

Fried Cabbage

1/2 pound bacon
1 tablespoon butter
1/2 large onion
1/2 green bell pepper
1 head green cabbage
2 tablespoons water
1 tablespoon sugar
1 teaspoon dried thyme
1 tablespoon whole grain mustard
1 tablespoon apple cider vinegar
Salt and pepper

Serves 6

Fry bacon until crispy. Remove the bacon from the pan and use the bacon grease to fry onion and bell pepper until tender.

Cut the head of cabbage into quarters and then start slicing the cabbage into shreds. Add sugar, 2 tablespoons water and thyme. Cover and fry, stirring occasionally, on medium heat until cabbage is al dente tender.

Stir in the butter, mustard and vinegar and season with salt and pepper. Crmble the reserved bacon, toss in and serve.

Fried Sauerkraut

8 slices bacon
4 tablespoons onions, diced
4 tablespoons butter
16 ounces sauerkraut
4 tablespoons sugar
Salt and pepper to taste

Serves 4

Drain sauerkraut in a colander. Fry bacon until crisp and set aside.

Sauté diced onions in bacon drippings until golden brown; add in the butter. Toss in the sauerkraut and the sugar and cook stirring frequently on medium heat until warm all the way through.

Salt and pepper to taste, top with the crispy fried bacon, crumbled.

Originally printed in the News-Leader, September 2006

Hoppin' John

2 cans cooked black eyed peas, drained
2 smoked ham hocks
2 medium onions, divided
3 cloves garlic
1 bay leaf
1 cup long-grain white rice
1 (14.5-ounce) can diced tomatoes with juice
1 red bell pepper, chopped
1/2 green bell pepper, chopped
3 ribs celery, chopped
1 jalapeno pepper, minced
3 teaspoons Creole seasoning
1/2 teaspoon dried thyme leaves
1 teaspoon cumin
4 green onions, sliced
1 teaspoon salt
Salt and pepper to taste

Serves 4

In a large pan combine the ham hocks and 4 cups water. Cut one of the onions in half and add it to the pot along with the garlic and bay leaf. Bring to a boil, reduce the heat to medium-low, and simmer gently for about 1 hour.

Remove the ham hocks and cut off the meat; dice and set aside.

Remove and discard the bay leaf, onion pieces and garlic.

Add the rice, peppers, celery and additional onion that has been diced, then cover and simmer until the rice is almost tender, about 15 minutes.

Add in the peas, tomatoes and their juices, Creole seasoning, thyme, cumin and salt. Cook until the rice is tender and the beans are hot, about 15 minutes.

Stir in the sliced green onions and the reserved diced ham. Adjust the seasonings and serve.

Indian Style Potatoes

3 tablespoons light olive oil
1/2 teaspoon whole cumin seeds
1 teaspoon crushed dried red
   chilies
1/2 teaspoon fenugreek seeds
1/2 teaspoon mustard seed
1/2 teaspoon fennel seed
1/2 teaspoon coriander seed
3 garlic cloves, roughly chopped
1 teaspoon fresh ginger, grated
2 onions, sliced
12 new potatoes, sliced
1/2 red bell pepper, seeded and
   sliced
1 fresh jalapeno pepper, seeded
   and sliced
Salt and pepper to taste

Serves 4

Heat the oil in a wok or a large heavy pan.

Add the cumin seed, dried chilies, mustard, fenugreek seeds, fennel seeds, chopped garlic and grated ginger.

Fry for about 1 minute, then add the sliced onions and fry gently for a further 5 minutes. Add the sliced potatoes, red bell peppers and green chilies. Mix together well.

Cover the pan tightly with a lid. Turn the heat to a very low setting and cook for about 7 minutes or until the potatoes are tender. Remove the lid, season and serve.

Originally printed in the News-Leader, January 2006

Nutty Wild Rice Sausage Stuffing

1 cup uncooked wild rice
2 cups water or chicken stock
1 1/4 cups uncooked long-grain
   rice
3 cups water or chicken stock
1 pound bulk sausage
2 tablespoons butter
2 celery ribs, sliced
1 cup button mushrooms, sliced
1 yellow onion, diced
Salt and black pepper to taste
1 cup chopped walnuts, toasted

Makes 12 servings

Prepare wild rice and long-grain rice separately accordingly using the water or chicken stock.

When the rice is done, toss together in large bowl and set aside.

In a skillet, cook sausage until well browned. Remove sausage and drain. Add to bowl with rice. Add butter to drippings remaining in skillet; add celery, mushrooms, onion, salt and pepper and cook until vegetables are tender. Remove from heat and add vegetables to rice mixture along with walnuts. Toss well to mix.

Place the stuffing in a baking dish and cover with foil. Bake at 350 degrees for one hour.

Originally printed in the News-Leader, November 2005

Pennsylvania Dutch Potato Stuffing

6 medium russet or Idaho
   potatoes, peeled and diced
8 slices white bread, diced small
1/4 cup butter
1/2 onion, diced
1 rib celery, sliced
2 eggs, beaten
1/2 cup sour cream or buttermilk
2 tablespoons chopped parsley
Salt and pepper to taste

Makes 8 servings

Lightly grease a 2-quart casserole. Boil potatoes for 15 minutes in lightly salted water until potatoes are tender, then drain. In a mixing bowl mash the potatoes and sour cream by hand until smooth.

In a small skillet melt butter; add onion and celery and sauté until vegetables are tender. Add mixture to potatoes and combine.

Add beaten eggs, parsley, salt and pepper to potato mixture and blend well. Add in the bread pieces and mix well. Place mixture in a buttered casserole dish and bake at 350 degrees, uncovered, 40 to 45 minutes.

Originally printed in the News-Leader, November 2005

Scalloped Cabbage

1 tablespoon butter for buttering
   the casserole dish
1 medium head green cabbage,
   cut into small wedges
2 tablespoons butter
2 tablespoons all-purpose flour
1/2 teaspoon salt
1 cup milk
1/2 tablespoon dry mustard
2/3 cup shredded cheddar cheese
1/2 teaspoon black pepper
1/2 cup crushed buttery round
   crackers or toasted bread
   crumbs

Serves 4

Preheat oven to 350 degrees. Butter a 2-quart casserole dish. Bring a large pot of salted water to a boil. Cook cabbage in boiling water until barely tender, about 10 minutes; drain well.

While the cabbage drains, melt butter in a small saucepan. Blend in flour and cook for about 3 to 4 minutes. Add in the milk, dry mustard, pepper and salt and bring to a boil, stirring all the while. After the milk has thickened, remove from the heat and let cool for a few minutes. Slowly add in the cheese a little at a time.

Transfer cabbage into the buttered casserole dish, and stir in cheese sauce. Sprinkle crumbs on top. Bake for 25 to 30 minutes or until top is browned.

Originally printed in the News-Leader, March 2004

Scalloped Potatoes

4 cups potatoes, sliced thin
1 cup yellow onions, sliced thin
5 tablespoons butter
5 tablespoons flour
2 1/2 cups milk
2 tablespoons Worcestershire
    sauce
1 teaspoon prepared yellow
    mustard
1 teaspoon salt
1 teaspoon pepper
1/2 teaspoon paprika
2 tablespoons red bell pepper,
    diced
2 cups cheddar cheese, shredded
2 cups ham, diced small
3/4 cup bread crumbs
4 tablespoons butter
2 teaspoons garlic powder

Serves 6 to 8

Cook potatoes and onions together in lightly salted water until tender, then drain well.

Melt 5 tablespoons butter in a saucepan. Add flour, stirring until blended.

Gradually stir in milk. Add Worcestershire, mustard, salt, pepper, paprika, garlic powder and bell pepper, stirring until thick. Place half of the potatoes and onions in a large, buttered 3-quart baking dish. Cover potatoes with half of the cheese. Add the ham and cover with remaining potatoes.

Pour the milk sauce over all. Sprinkle remaining cheese over top.

Sprinkle crumbs on top and dot with butter. Bake in preheated 350-degree oven until cheese is melted, and the top is browned.

Originally printed in the News-Leader, April 2006

Spam Fried Rice

2 tablespoons vegetable oil, divided
2 eggs, beaten
1 can Spam, diced
1/4 cup carrot, diced
1/4 cup green onions, chopped
1/4 cup mushrooms, sliced
1/4 cup frozen peas
1/4 cup red bell pepper, diced
1 garlic clove, minced
4 cups rice, cooked and cooled
2 tablespoons sesame oil
4 tablespoons soy sauce

Serves 4

In large skillet, heat 1 tablespoon of oil. Add eggs and cook until done, then remove from the skillet.

In same skillet, heat remaining 1 tablespoon oil. Cook the carrots, green onions, garlic and bell pepper 4 minutes or until vegetables are tender. Add in spam and cook for another 2 minutes.

Stir in the rice, peas, chopped egg and sesame oil. Stir in the soy sauce.

Originally printed in the News-Leader, October 2005

Spicy Baked Beans

1 (15-ounce) can black beans
1 (28-ounce) can baked beans
1 (15-ounce) can navy beans
1 large onion, chopped
1 medium bell pepper, chopped
1 jalapeno, minced
1/4 cup ketchup
2 tablespoons brown sugar,
   packed
2 tablespoons prepared mustard
2 teaspoons Worcestershire sauce
1/2 teaspoon garlic powder
2 teaspoons ground chipotle
   peppers
4 slices bacon

Makes 6 Servings

Preheat oven to 350 degrees. Combine all ingredients, including liquid from beans, in baking pan. Stir gently but thoroughly until all ingredients are mixed well.

Lay bacon strips across the top of baking pan. Bake 1 hour, or until the mixture is bubbly.

Originally printed in the News-Leader, June 2005

Spicy Corn Casserole

4 ounces chorizo sausage
1 small onion
2 boxes Jiffy cornbread mix
1 cup sour cream
2 eggs
1/2 cup salsa
1 small can fire-roasted chilies
1 cup shredded cheddar cheese

Serves 6

Cook the chorizo sausage and the onions together in a sauté pan until the onions are tender. Allow this mixture to cool.

Combine the remaining ingredients with the cooked and chilled sausage and onions and pour into an oiled casserole dish.

Bake in a 325 degree oven for 45 to 60 minutes or until firm in the middle.

Stewed Rhubarb - Grandma Andre's Recipe

2 pounds rhubarb
1 cup sugar
1 cup water

Serves 6

Cut the leaves off the rhubarb and wash the stalks thoroughly. Cut stalks in 1-inch pieces, add the sugar and water. Cover kettle and cook slowly until rhubarb is tender. Chill and serve plain or on buttered bread.

Toasted Pecan, Cider and Cornbread Stuffing

3 tablespoons vegetable oil
2 celery stalks, minced
1 onion, minced
2 cups pecans, toasted and
    chopped
2 teaspoons ground sage
1 pound prepared cornbread
    stuffing mix
2 1/2 cups apple cider
6 tablespoons butter

Makes 8 servings

Heat the oil in a large skillet and sauté the celery and onion translucent, about 10 minutes. On a cookie sheet, toast pecans 5 to 7 minutes at 325 degrees.

In a large bowl, mix the sautéed vegetables, pecans and sage together with the cornbread stuffing.

In a small saucepan, combine the cider and butter; and heat until the butter is completely melted. Pour over the stuffing mixture, mixing well. Season the stuffing with salt and pepper.

Bake stuffing in buttered casserole and bake at 325 degrees until hot and crusty, about 45 to 60 minutes.

Originally printed in the News-Leader, November 2005

Twice Baked Sweet Potatoes

4 sweet potatoes
2 tablespoons salad oil
1/4 cup brown sugar
2 tablespoons butter
1/2 teaspoon vanilla extract
1/4 cup Kahlua or other coffee
    liquor
1/2 teaspoon salt
1/2 teaspoon pepper
1/3 cup pecans, chopped and
    toasted

Serves 4

Preheat oven to 350 degrees. Rub sweet potato skins with oil and bake in preheated oven for 1 hour.

When cooked through, cut potatoes in half and scoop flesh into the bowl.

Add in remaining ingredients and mix well.

Spoon the mixture back into potato skins.

Return to the oven and bake for 10 minutes.

Originally printed in the News-Leader, November 2006

Vegetarian Baked Black Beans

2 (15-ounce) cans black beans,
  rinsed and drained
1 (8-ounce) can tomato sauce
1 cup onion, chopped
1 red bell pepper, chopped
1 yellow bell pepper, chopped
1/2 cup chili sauce
1 tablespoon maple syrup
2 teaspoons chili powder
1/2 teaspoon powdered ginger
1/8 teaspoon ground red pepper

Serves 6

Put all ingredients in a bowl and stir well. Put into a 2 quart casserole that has been sprayed with nonstick spray.

Cover and bake 1 hour at 350 degrees.

Originally printed in the News-Leader, June 2005

Chef Lou multitasking

Family Favorites

Basic Lemonade Syrup

1 1/2 cups sugar
1/2 cup boiling water
Zest of 1 lemon
1 1/2 cups lemon juice

Makes 6 servings

Dissolve sugar into boiling water. Remove from heat and add in the lemon zest and juice. Refrigerate for later use.

To make a glass of lemonade, mix 1/4 cup of the syrup to 3/4 cup of cold water.

Originally printed in the News-Leader, June 2006

Brazilian Lemonade

2 lemons
1/2 cup sugar
3 tablespoons sweetened
   condensed milk
3 cups water
Ice

Yield: 1

Wash lemons thoroughly. Cut off the ends and slice into eight wedges. Place lemons in a blender with the sugar, sweetened condensed milk, water and ice. Blend in an electric blender, pulsing 5 times. Strain through a fine mesh strainer to remove rinds. Serve over ice.

Originally printed in the News-Leader, June 2006

Chef Lou's Bean Stew

3 cups red beans, soaked overnight
3 cups pinto beans, soaked
   overnight
3 pieces bacon
1 large green bell pepper, diced
1 large yellow onion, diced
2 cloves garlic, minced
1 cup seasoned ham, diced
1 pound smoked sausage, sliced
1 large tomato, chopped
4 cups water
2 cups chicken stock
2 tablespoons garlic powder
2 bay leaves
2 teaspoons liquid smoke
Salt and pepper to taste

Serves 6

Place the soaked and drained beans into a slow cooker and add the pepper/onion mix.

Cook the bacon until crisp then remove from the pan. Sauté the onions and peppers in the bacon grease until they start to caramelize and develop a nice brown color.

In the same skillet sauté the ham to once again develop some color and taste. Add this to the beans. Do the same thing with the smoked sausage and add it to the pot. Add some water to the caramelizing skillet to deglaze it and add this liquid to the cooker. Add in any remaining liquids, garlic and seasonings. Bring the beans to a boil, then reduce to just below a simmer and cook for 4 hours.

As the ham, sausage and possibly chicken stock contain higher levels of salt, do not add salt until you are ready for the final tasting.

Originally printed in the News-Leader, January 2005

Chocolate Pie with a Crunchy Crust

Tart pan or 10-inch pie pan
9 ounces good semi-sweet
   chocolate chips
1 1/2 cups heavy cream
2 eggs
1 egg yolk
2 teaspoons almond extract

Crunchy Crust:
1/3 cup sugar
1 1/2 cups blanched almonds
1 egg white
Melted butter for tart pan

Serves 10

Crunchy Crust:
Grind the sugar and blanched almonds together in a food processor. In a medium bowl, whisk the egg white until frothy.

Transfer the ground almond and sugar mixture from the food processor to the beaten egg white. Stir the mixture to form a stiff paste. Shape it into a ball, wrap in plastic wrap tightly and chill until firm, about 30 minutes. Brush the tart pan with the melted butter. Lightly flour the work surface, then use a rolling pin to flatten out the dough to fit the tart pan. Carefully, transfer the dough to the tart pan.

Press the dough into the bottom of the pan and along the sides. Blind bake the shell in a 350 degree oven until lightly browned or about 8 to 10 minutes then let cool.

Filling:
In a saucepan, bring the cream to a boil and pour over the chocolate in a bowl. Add in the extract and whisk the chocolate, extract and cream together until the chocolate has melted completely. Set the mixture aside to cool slightly.

Put the eggs and the egg yolk into another bowl and whisk them together until mixed. Lightly whisk the chocolate and cream mixture into the beaten eggs.

Pour the filling into the cooled shell. Put the tart on a baking sheet and bake until filling holds together when the pan is lightly shaken, 15-20 minutes. Allow the tart to cool on a rack before removing from the pan and serving.

Originally printed in the News-Leader, February 2006

Cranberry Catsup

4 cups cranberries, fresh
1 cup onion, finely chopped
2 cups water
4 cups sugar
2 cups vinegar, white
1 teaspoon pepper
1 tablespoon salt
1 tablespoon cinnamon
1 tablespoon allspice
1 tablespoon celery seeds
2 tablespoons cloves, ground
1 tablespoon ground ginger

Makes 2 Pints

In 3-quart heavy pan, combine all of the ingredients. Bring to a boil, then reduce the heat, cover and simmer for about 15 minutes.

Puree mixture with a food processor or blender. Be careful with blenders and hot items. Continue to simmer the berry spice puree until it is nicely thickened. It will take about 30 minutes. Stir occasionally to prevent sticking as the mixture thickens.

Remove from the heat and store refrigerated for several months.

Originally printed in the News-Leader, November 2005

Creamy Chai Tea

2 cups water
4 tablespoons ginger, diced
1 cinnamon stick
4 whole cloves
1 teaspoon cardamom powder
2 tablespoons vanilla extract
1/4 teaspoon nutmeg
2 tablespoons sugar
1/4 cup honey
3 Darjeeling tea bags
2 cups milk

Serve 4 hot or cold

Bring water to a boil and add in all of the remaining ingredients except for the milk.

Reduce the heat to a simmer and cook for about 5 minutes stirring occasionally.

Add in the milk and bring back to a boil.

Remove from the heat and strain through a fine mesh strainer.

Originally printed in the News-Leader, August 2007

Freezer Coleslaw

1 head cabbage, shredded
1 green bell pepper, chopped
1 onion, chopped
1 red bell pepper, chopped
2 cups sugar
2 teaspoons salt
1 teaspoon celery seed
1/2 cup apple cider vinegar
1 cup water

Serves 6

Toss all of the vegetables into a large bowl.

Mix remaining ingredients in saucepan and bring to a boil. Boil for 2 to 3 minutes. Let cool. Pour over vegetables and mix well.

Pack in airtight plastic freezer container and freeze. This slaw is also good after a night's chilling in the fridge.

Originally printed in the News-Leader, August 2005

Fried Corn

1 pound fresh sweet corn
1 half stick butter
1 half red pepper, diced
2 ounces onion, chopped
1/2 cup milk
2 tablespoons sugar
Salt and black pepper to taste

Serves 4

Cut the corn from the cob and scrape the cobs with the dull edge of a knife to squeeze out any remaining milk.

Melt the butter in a frying pan. Add the red pepper and onion and sauté for 5 minutes. Add the corn, corn milk and sugar, and cook over medium heat for 15 minutes, stirring frequently.

Frozen Strawberry Lemonade Recipe

4 large lemons
1 half-pint carton strawberries,
    cut into slices and hulled, if
    desired
3/8 cup granulated sugar
3 cups cold, sparkling water
Lemon slices and fresh mint
    leaves, for garnish
Ice cubes

Makes 6 servings

Wash and squeeze the juice from the lemons, reserving the lemon skins. Strain the juice into a pitcher. Add the lemon skins and sugar. Using a spoon, crush the lemon skins into the juice and sugar to release the oils. Add the sliced strawberries and sparkling water and stir to mix well. Pour all the ingredients into a blender, add ice cubes, and blend until smooth. Serve in chilled glasses and garnish with lemon slices and fresh mint leaves.

If you do not have or don't like sparkling water, plain water will do.

Originally printed in the News-Leader, June 2006

Grilled Potato Salad

2 pounds baby red potatoes, quartered
1 red bell pepper, sliced thin
1 green bell pepper, sliced thin
1 red onion, sliced thin
4 green onions
3/4 cup bacon crumbles
Parsley, finely chopped
1 tablespoon Creole mustard
2 tablespoons white wine vinegar
2 cups mayonnaise
1 tablespoon garlic powder
1 teaspoon dry mustard
Salt and pepper to taste

Serves 4

Blanch potatoes in boiling water until tender but still firm, then drain. On a preheated grill, grill the peppers, red onion and green onion until they start to caramelize. Remove peppers and onions, then dice.

Toss potatoes with olive oil and toss onto hot grill grates. Grill for about 10 minutes or until potatoes have nice grill markings.

Mix potatoes with peppers, onions and remaining ingredients and chill for service.

Homemade Peach Lemonade

2 fresh peaches; peeled and cubed
4 cups water
1 cup sugar
3/4 cup fresh lemon juice

Serves 4

Bring the peaches, sugar and water to a boil, then simmer until the sugar is dissolved, about 10 minutes. Allow the mixture to cool, then strain through a sieve, pressing to extract as much juice as possible. Stir in the lemon juice and serve in tall glasses over ice.

Originally printed in the News-Leader, June 2006

Homestyle Cooked Eggnog

6 eggs
1 cup sugar
2 cups milk
2 cups heavy cream or
  half-and-half
2 teaspoons vanilla extract
1/4 teaspoon ground cinnamon
1/2 teaspoon ground nutmeg

6 servings

In saucepan, beat together the eggs and sugar until smooth. Stir in 2 cups milk. Cook over medium low heat, stirring frequently to prevent scorching. Cook until mixture is thick enough to coat a metal spoon and reaches 160 degrees on a food thermometer. Remove from heat.

Slowly add the 2 cups whipping cream or half-and-half while whisking together until smooth. Add vanilla, cinnamon and nutmeg and combine until incorporated.
Pour into a container and cover and refrigerate until thoroughly chilled-several hours or overnight. Serve garnished with whipped cream and nutmeg.

Originally printed in the News-Leader, December 2005

Mom's Holiday Ham

1 (10 -12-pound) sugar-cured,
   fully cooked ham
1-pound box dark brown sugar
2 cups mustard
1-liter bottle Coca-Cola

Serves 10 to 12

Place the ham in a baking pan. Using a sharp knife cut a criss-cross pattern on the outside skin about 1/8-inch of an inch deep. Rub the mustard all over the ham and into the cuts. Pack on the brown sugar all over the ham and on top of the mustard and into the cracks as well.

Pour half of the Coca-Cola over the top of the ham and pour the rest into the baking pan. Bake ham for a total of 16 minutes per pound at 350 degrees.

Remove ham from oven and allow it to stand for at least 15 minutes before transferring to serving platter. Skim fat from pan juices and serve with the ham.

Originally printed in the News-Leader, April 2006

Mom's Hot Chocolate

1/2 cup granulated sugar
1/3 cup hot water
1/4 cup cocoa powder
4 cups milk
1 tablespoon butter
1/8 teaspoon salt
1 teaspoon vanilla extract

Makes 4 servings

Mix cocoa, butter, sugar, water and salt in a saucepan. Over medium heat, stir constantly until mixture boils. Cook, stirring constantly, for 1 minute. Reduce the heat and stir in the milk. Bring back up to a simmer. Remove from heat and blend in the vanilla.

Serve immediately.

Mom's Strawberry Layer Salad

1 (6-ounce) package strawberry
   Jell-O
2 cups boiling water
1 large package frozen
   strawberries
1 large can crushed pineapple,
   drained
3 large bananas, mashed
2 cups sour cream

Serves 4

Mix half of the fruit with half of the Jell-O and let set up. When firm, spread with layer of sour cream. Pour remaining fruit and Jell-O mixture over sour cream. Cover with plastic wrap and refrigerate till set.

Originally printed in the News-Leader, December 2003

More Like Mom's Slaw

1 head of cabbage, finely shredded
1/4 head red cabbage, finely
   shredded
1 medium green bell pepper,
   finely chopped
1 medium onion, minced
2 carrots, grated

Dressing:
1 cup sugar
1 teaspoon salt
1/2 teaspoon black pepper
1/3 cup mayonnaise
1 teaspoon dry mustard
2 teaspoons celery seed
1 cup apple cider vinegar
1/2 cup milk

8 to 10 servings

Combine coleslaw vegetable ingredients--chopped cabbages, chopped bell pepper, chopped onions and grated carrots--in a large serving bowl.

Combine remaining ingredients in a bowl and stir until the sugar is dissolved.

Pour over vegetables and toss well. Cover and chill.

Originally printed in the News-Leader, August 2005

Mother-In-Law's French Silk Pie

1/2 cup butter
3/4 cup sugar
2 squares unsweetened chocolate,
   melted
2 eggs
1 (4.5-ounce) tub Cool Whip
1 baked pie shell

Serves 8

Cream together butter and sugar until light and fluffy, then stir in the melted chocolate. Add one egg at a time, beating on high speed for 5 minutes each. Fold the Cool Whip into chocolate mixture and pour into pie shell. Refrigerate until set.

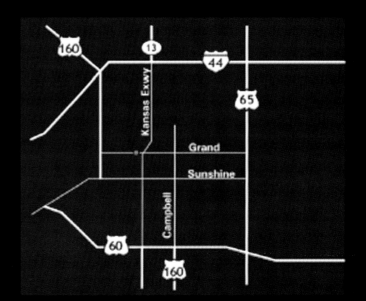

Mother-In-Law's Porcupine Meatballs

1 pound hamburger
1 slice of bread, for crumbs
1 medium onion, diced
1 green pepper, diced
1 egg
1 cup rice, cooked

Sauce:
14 ounces ketchup
14 ounces water
3/4 cup brown sugar

Serves 4

Mix the cooked rice, diced onion and green pepper with the hamburger and form into large meatballs (about 2-1/2 inches in diameter). Place meatballs into hot pan or electric skillet. Mix sauce ingredients and pour over meatballs. Cook for one hour on medium to medium-high heat, turning the meatballs occasionally until done.

My Basic Chicken Wings

4 cups Franks Red Hot sauce
1/2 cup Tabasco green sauce
1/4 cup Tabasco sauce
1/4 cup Cholula Mexican hot sauce
1 cup Italian dressing
2 tablespoons red pepper flakes, if desired for heat
3 pounds chicken drummettes
1/2 cup butter

Serves 4-6

Combine first five ingredients up to chicken wings and mix well. Remove about one third of the sauce and set aside. Place chicken wings into a plastic bag with remaining sauce, seal and let marinate for 24 hours.

Remove chicken wings from marinade, place on a rack and bake in a preheated 450-degree oven for about 20 minutes. Heat a skillet, add in the reserved sauce and the butter and bring to a simmer. Add in the chicken wings from the oven and cook for about 5 minutes, stirring to coat the sauce evenly.

My BBQ Sauce

1 pint ketchup
1 cup puréed fruit (peaches, apricots or pineapple, etc.)
1/4 cup apple cider vinegar
1/4 cup brown sugar
1/4 cup honey
1/4 cup ground cumin
1/4 cup Worcestershire sauce
3 tablespoons liquid smoke
3 tablespoons ground mustard
3 tablespoons red pepper flakes
Salt and pepper to taste

Makes approximately 1 quart

Combine all of the ingredients in a sauce pan and simmer for 1 hour.

You may add more honey, vinegar or red pepper flakes to suit your own taste.

Originally printed in the News-Leader, September 2003

My Favorite Fruitcake

1 pound dried apples
1 pound pitted dates
1/2 pound pecans, lightly toasted
1/2 pound blanched almonds
1/4 pound walnuts, lightly
  toasted
1 tablespoon orange zest
2 cups apple schnapps or Triple-
  Sec (orange-flavored liquor)
1/2 cup Amaretto liqueur
1/4 cup dark corn syrup
1 1/2 cups unsalted butter
1 1/4 cups firmly packed light
  brown sugar
8 large eggs
1 tablespoon vanilla extract
1 tablespoon almond extract
2 cups all-purpose flour
1/2 teaspoon salt
2 teaspoons baking powder
1 teaspoon ground cinnamon
1 teaspoon ground allspice
1/2 teaspoon ground mace
Additional Amaretto for basting

Makes 1 fruitcake

All the fruits, zest and nuts are ground as finely as possible in a food grinder. Place the fruit/nut mixture in a large bowl. Add triple sec, amaretto and corn syrup. Mix well, cover and set aside for at least 1 week.

Baking day arrives! Grease and line the base and sides of one 12x12-inch square or round baking pan with brown paper and grease well with shortening.

Preheat the oven to 275 degrees.

Cream together the butter and sugar until well blended. Add eggs, one at a time, beating after each addition. Add vanilla and almond essence. Sift the flour with the salt and spices and fold them into the butter and sugar mixture.

Stir in the fruit mixture a little at a time until it is evenly blended. Spoon the cake mixture into the prepared pan.

Bake for approximately 2 hours until the cake is a rich brown color and feels firm to the touch. A cake tester inserted in the center should show no visible sign of raw batter though it may be sticky from the fruit (be sure not to over bake).

Leave to cool completely in the pan before turning out onto a wire rack. When the cake is cold, wrap it well in two layers of cheese-cloth.

Soak the cheesecloth with some of the amaretto. Wrap the moist cloth in plastic wrap then in silver foil, or keep it in an airtight container, and store in a cool dry place.

Periodically, brush more amaretto on the cheesecloth if it dries out.

Old Fashioned Indiana Lemon Shake Up

1 cup sugar
1 quart water
6 lemons

Makes 12 servings

Mix sugar in water. Cut the lemons in half. Juice half of the lemons with a juicer. Put half of the rinds from those lemons into a 2-quart bowl that has a firm-fitting lid. Juice the other half of the lemons with a juicer and discard the other half of the rind.

Fill bowl one-quarter of the way with ice. Add the lemon juice, sugar water, and rind. Apply lid to bowl and shake for 10 or 15 seconds. Pour into 12-ounce serving cup.

Originally printed in the News-Leader, June 2006

Perfection Salad

1 package lime Jell-O
1 package lemon Jell-O
1 can crushed pineapple, drained
2 carrots, shredded fine
1 cup cabbage, shredded fine
Mayonnaise to garnish

Makes 4 servings

Prepare the Jell-O per the directions on the label. Add in the carrot, cabbage and pineapple.

Refrigerate until set. Serve with a dollop of mayonnaise

Originally printed in the News-Leader, December 2003

Perfectly Simple Lemonade

3 1/2 cups water
1 cup fresh-squeezed lemon juice
   (about 4 to 6 lemons)
1/2 to 1 cup of granulated sugar
   (depending on your taste)

Makes 4 servings

Mix water and lemon juice, dissolving the sugar into the mixture. Chill.

Originally printed in the News-Leader, June 2006

Pineapple Wafer Ice Box Cake

3 cups crushed vanilla wafers
1/2 cup butter
1 1/2 cups powdered sugar
2 eggs
1 cup whipping cream
1 cup crushed pineapple, well drained
1/2 cup shredded coconut
1/2 cup toasted pecans

Makes 1 cake

In a 9x13-inch pan, sprinkle 2 cups of the crushed vanilla wafers.

Cream together the butter, powdered sugar and eggs. Place over crumbs. Add in the pecans and the coconut. Whip the cream until firm and fold in pineapple.

Spoon this over the pecans and coconut. Top with the remaining crushed wafers.

Refrigerate overnight to set up before serving.

Rhubarb Strawberry Lemonade

4 cups water
1/2 pound rhubarb, diced
1 cup sugar
4 slices lemon
2 (1-inch-long) pieces of lemon zest
1 teaspoon vanilla
2 cups strawberries, sliced
1 cup fresh lemon juice

Makes 4 servings

In a saucepan stir together the water, the rhubarb, the sugar, 2 strips of the zest and the vanilla. Bring the mixture to a boil, stirring until the sugar is dissolved and simmer it, covered, for 8 minutes. Stir in the strawberries and boil the mixture, covered, for 2 minutes.

Let the mixture cool and strain it through a coarse sieve set over a pitcher, pressing hard on the solids. Stir in the lemon juice, pour over ice and garnish with lemon zest and wedges

Originally printed in the News-Leader, June 2006

Standard BBQ Rub

1 cup paprika
1 cup brown sugar
1/4 cup garlic powder
1/4 cup onion powder
3 tablespoons ground thyme
3 tablespoons ground oregano
3 tablespoons kosher salt
2 tablespoons ground red pepper
2 tablespoons black pepper

Yield: 3 to 4 cups

These are made to taste, but this tends to be the one I like.

Combine all of the ingredients and store in an airtight container. Use as much as your taste demands then store the rest in the container for up to six months.

Originally printed in the News-Leader, September 2003

Kid Friendly

All-American Parfaits

2 cups boiling water
1 (4-serving size) package Berry
Blue Jell-O
1 (4-serving size) package
strawberry Jell-O
2 cups cold water
1 tub (8 ounces) Cool Whip
whipped topping, thawed or
canned whipped cream
1 cup strawberries, halved
1 cup blueberries

Serves 4

Stir boiling water into gelatin in large bowl at least 2 minutes until completely dissolved. Stir in cold water. Refrigerate 4 hours or until firm.

Spoon one flavor of Jell-O into parfait glass, top with whipped cream and add on the berries. Add on another flavor of Jell-O and repeat the process.

Basic Tomato Sauce

1/4 cup extra-virgin olive oil
1 onion, chopped in 1/4-inch dice
4 garlic cloves, thinly sliced
1 tablespoon dried thyme
1/2 medium carrot, finely
shredded
3 cups tomato, diced
2 cups tomato puree
1 cup tomato paste
Salt and pepper

Makes 6 cups

In a 3-quart saucepan, heat the olive oil over moderate heat. Add the onion and garlic and cook until soft and light golden brown, 8 to 10 minutes.

Add the thyme and carrot and cook 5 minutes more until the carrot is quite soft.

Add the tomatoes, tomato paste and juice and bring to a boil, stirring often. Lower the heat and simmer for 30 minutes. Season with salt and serve with the pasta noodles of your choice.

Caesar Salad

1 large head romaine lettuce
1 cup olive oil
3 cups French bread
2 large cloves garlic
1 teaspoon Worcestershire sauce
1 teaspoon dry mustard
2 tablespoons lemon juice
1 teaspoon fresh ground black pepper
1 teaspoon coarse ground salt
1/2 cup grated parmesan cheese
1/4 cup parmesan cheese, shredded or shaved

Serves 4

Trim the romaine lettuce of bruised or browned leaves, then cut into 1-1/2-inch pieces. Wash and drain the lettuce, pat it dry and refrigerate for 30 minutes to crisp the leaves.

To make the croutons, cut the bread into cubes, drizzle with the olive oil and bake in a 350-degree oven for 20 minutes or until browned.

Peel the garlic cloves and put in a large salad bowl. Mash the cloves against the sides of the bowl with the back of a wooden spoon. Rub the pieces against the bowl until they begin to disintegrate. Remove most of the mashed garlic from the bowl and discard.

Add the dry mustard, Worcestershire sauce, lemon juice, and black pepper and blend well. Slowly drizzle in the remaining olive oil mixing with a wire whisk until a creamy mayonnaise-type dressing forms.

Add the lettuce, croutons, parmesan cheese and salt. Toss everything together and serve directly from the salad bowl.

Cannoli

6 cannoli shells
8 ounces cream cheese
3/4 cup powdered sugar
1/2 cup strawberry jam
1 teaspoon orange zest
1/2 cup chocolate chips
1/2 cup half-and-half

Serves 6

Mix the cheese with the sugar and the jam until it is very smooth.

Using a piping bag, pipe the filling into the cannoli shells.

Heat the half-and-half in a microwave until boiling and add in the chocolate, stirring until smooth.

Drizzle the chocolate over the cannolis and decorate with powdered sugar.

Cheesy Quiche

6 large eggs
1 cup sliced ham
3/4 cup Swiss cheese, grated
3/4 cup cheddar cheese, grated
1/2 cup ricotta cheese
1 cup half-and-half
2 teaspoons onion, finely chopped
2 teaspoons fresh parsley, finely
  chopped
1/4 teaspoon salt
1/8 teaspoon pepper
1 (9-inch) store-bought unbaked
  pie shell

Serves 4

Preheat oven to 375 degrees. Place all the cheeses and ham in the pie shell and gently mix together. In a medium bowl, place all remaining ingredients and mix until smooth (use a blender if you like).

Pour the new mixture in the pie shell on top of the cheeses. Bake for 20 minutes. Lower the oven temperature to 350 degrees and continue baking for 35 to 40 more minutes, or until a knife inserted in center comes out clean.

Remove from oven. Allow to cool 5 to 10 minutes before slicing. Serve warm.

Cinnamon Orange French Toast

4 eggs
3 teaspoons sugar, optional
1 teaspoon salt
1 cup milk
1/2 cup orange juice
3 teaspoons cinnamon
10 to 12 slices French bread
Butter
Maple syrup or other syrup

Serves 4

Break eggs into a wide, shallow bowl and whisk in sugar, salt, orange juice, cinnamon and milk.

Over medium-low heat, heat griddle or skillet coated with a thin layer of butter.

Place the bread slices, one at a time, into the bowl or plate, letting slices soak up egg mixture for a few seconds, then carefully turn to coat the other side. Soak/coat only as many slices as you will be cooking at one time.

Transfer bread slices to griddle or skillet, heating slowly until bottom is golden brown. Turn and brown the other side. Serve French toast hot with butter and syrup.

Giant Brownie Ice Cream Sandwich

2 packages fudge brownie mix,
   (approx 8-inch square pan size)
1 tablespoon shortening, for pan
   greasing
4 cups chocolate chip mint ice
   cream, softened
1/2 cup mini semi-sweet chocolate
   chips
1/2 cup chocolate sauce from the
   store
1 cup whipped topping for garnish
4 sprigs fresh mint for garnish

Serves 8

Prepare the brownie mixes according to package directions. Pour into two greased 8-inch square baking pans. Bake at 350 degrees for 25 to 30 minutes or until a toothpick inserted near the center comes out clean. Cool for 10 minutes before removing from pans to wire racks to cool completely.

Freeze the brownies for 2 hours or until easy to handle. Remove the brownies from the freezer and spoon ice cream on top of one brownie layer. Top the ice cream with a drizzle of chocolate sauce. Place the second brownie layer on top of the ice cream and wrap in plastic wrap; freeze until set.

When ready to serve, remove from the freezer and cut into square-or triangle-shaped serving pieces. Allow to thaw for about 10 minutes before serving. Top with any remaining chocolate sauce, chocolate chips, whipped cream and mint.

Hannah s Chocolate Strawberry Parfait

1 (3-ounce) package of strawberry
   Jell-O
1 envelope Dream Whip
1/2 cup chocolate milk
1/2 teaspoon vanilla
Chocolate sprinkles
4 strawberries, sliced

Serves 4

Make the Jell-O per the recipe on the box and chill to the set but not firm stage.

Prepare the Dream Whip using the chocolate milk and vanilla. Layer the Jell-O and Dream Whip in a parfait or similar tall glass in alternating layers.

Top each parfait with the sliced strawberry and a sprinkle of the chocolate.

Originally printed in the News-Leader, August 2005

Hannah's Homemade Ranch Dressing

1 teaspoon garlic powder
1 cup mayonnaise
  (we like Hellman's)
1/2 cup buttermilk
2 tablespoons fresh parsley, minced
2 tablespoons fresh chives, minced
1 green onion, thinly sliced
1 teaspoon white vinegar
2 tablespoons water, for thinning
1 teaspoon lemon juice
Salt and pepper to taste

Makes 2 cups

In a medium bowl, whisk in the garlic powder, mayonnaise, buttermilk, parsley, chives, green onion, vinegar, and lemon juice. Salt and pepper to taste.

To make this more fun for the kids, we put 6 drops of blue food coloring into the dressing.

Homemade Baked Chicken Fingers

2 chicken breasts, trimmed
2 cups corn flakes, crushed
1/2 teaspoon paprika
2 teaspoons salt
1 teaspoon black pepper
1 cup buttermilk
3 tablespoons honey

Serves 4

Combine buttermilk and honey. Cut the chicken into equal strips and place them into the buttermilk and honey for 20 minutes. Combine the corn flakes, pepper, salt and paprika in a plastic bag.

Place the chicken strips into the bag with the dry ingredients and shake to coat. Place the strips on a baking sheet sprayed with nonstick cooking spray and bake in a 350-degree oven for about 20 minutes.

Homemade Scalloped Corn

1 tablespoon butter, for buttering
  dish
1 can cream style corn
1 can whole kernel corn
1 package Jiffy corn mix
1/2 cup Ritz cracker crumbs
1 cup sour cream
3 tablespoons sugar
Pinch salt
1 teaspoon pepper
2 tablespoons butter

Serves 4

Butter an approximately 10x10-inch baking dish.

Combine all ingredients but try not to over mix.

You can add a little milk if the batter is too stiff.

Pour into the buttered baking dish and top with 2 tablespoons of butter.

Bake at 350 degrees for 1 hour or until set in the middle.

Jell-O Ice Cream Pie

1 pint vanilla ice cream
1 cup fresh fruit, chopped
  (like strawberries)
1 (3-ounce) package of Jell-O,
  any flavor (flavor should match
  the fruit)
1 cup hot water
1 graham cracker crust pie shell

Serves 8

Dissolve Jell-O in 1 cup of hot water.

Mix ice cream into the Jell-O and stir until completely dissolved.

Blend in fruit.

Pour into a pie shell and refrigerate until set.

Originally printed in the News-Leader, August 2005

Jell-O Pizza

4 (3-ounce) packages Jell-O,
  any flavor
2 1/2 cups boiling water
1 cup Cool Whip
3 cups fresh fruit (washed)

Serves 4

Pour gelatin into bowl. Add 2-1/2 cups boiling water to gelatin, stirring until gelatin is completely dissolved, about 2 minutes. Place a 14-inch pizza pan on a cookie sheet or baking tray for stability. Pour Jell-O into the pizza pan. Put pan into refrigerator to chill until firm. Remove pan from refrigerator when ready to serve.

Put about 1 inch of warm water in sink and dip just bottom of pan into warm water for 15 seconds. Spread whipped topping over gelatin pizza, leaving about 1 inch of space around outside edge of gelatin for pizza "crust."

Top pizza with fruit and cut pizza into wedges.

Originally printed in the News-Leader, August 2005

Jell-O Smoothie

8 ounces prepared Jell-O
  (any flavor)
8 ounces milk
8 ounces sherbet,
  (flavor of your choice)

Serves 2

Prepare Jell-O and place in the fridge until set.

In a blender combine the set Jell-O and other ingredients and blend until smooth.

Top with whipped cream.

Originally printed in the News-Leader, August 2005

Meatballs

1 pound ground beef
4 tablespoons dry bread crumbs
1 egg
4 tablespoons parmesan cheese
1 teaspoon salt
1/2 teaspoon black pepper
2 teaspoons dried Italian seasoning

Serves 4

Mix together all meatball ingredients in a bowl.

Form into balls 1-1/2 inch wide.

Bake on cookie sheet at 375 degrees for 25 minutes.

Mint Chocolate Chip Ice Cream

2 cups heavy cream
2 cups milk
1-2 teaspoons mint extract
2 teaspoons vanilla extract
1 1/4 cups sugar
1 cup mini semi-sweet chocolate chips
3-5 drops green food coloring (optional)
Pinch of salt

Serves 4

Whisk together milk and sugar. Add cream, extracts, salt, and food coloring. Pour the milk-cream mixture into ice cream machine and process according to manufacturer s instructions.

While the ice cream is in the machine, put 1/4 cup chocolate chips into a blender or food processor and chop until mixture is crumbly. Set aside.

In the last 5 minutes of the cycle, add in the whole and chopped-up chocolate chips. When the ice cream is finished, spoon into freezable container and allow to freeze for 20 to 30 minutes, depending on desired consistency.

Originally printed in the News-Leader, August 2007

Nutty Fruit Salad

2 cups Granny Smith apples, unpeeled and diced
1/2 cup celery, diced
1/3 cup pecans, chopped
3 heaping tablespoonfuls mayonnaise
1 tablespoon honey
Dash lemon juice
1/2 cup red grapes, sliced
1/4 cup dried cranberries

Serves 4

Stir together the mayonnaise, honey and lemon juice. Combine all ingredients together and chill until ice-cold.

If desired, serve on lettuce and garnish with grapes or cherries.

Peach Jell-O Pie

1 prepared graham cracker crust
1 cup sugar
1/4 cup cornstarch
1 (12-ounce) can of 7sUP
1 (3-ounce) package peach Jell-O
5 large fresh peaches, peeled and
   sliced
Cool Whip

Serves 8

In a small saucepan, mix together sugar, cornstarch and 7UP. Cook until thick.

Cool 5 minutes and add the package of dry peach Jell-O.

Cool 10 minutes and pour over sliced peaches. Pour into pie shell. Chill and top with Cool Whip.

Originally printed in the News-Leader, August 2005

Peanut Butter Cereal Treats

4 cups of your favorite breakfast
   cereal
1/2 cup sugar
1/2 cup honey
1/2 cup peanut butter

Makes about 36 (1-1/2-inch) bars

Line an 8- or 9-inch square baking pan with plastic wrap. Pour cereal into large bowl.

In medium saucepan combine sugar and honey syrup. Stirring ccasionally, bring to boil over medium heat and boil 1 minute. Remove from heat.

Stir in peanut butter until smooth. Pour over cereal; stir to coat. Press evenly into prepared pan. Cool about 15 minutes. Invert onto cutting board; remove plastic wrap. Cut into bars.

You can make this in a microwave by combining the sugar, honey and peanut butter in a microwave-safe bowl. Microwave on high for 4 minutes or until mixture is smooth and sugar is dissolved. You will want to stir this a couple of times as it cooks.

Mix in the peanut butter until smooth. Pour the mixture over the cereal and mix together.

Press the coated cereal into the pan until even. When cool turn the pan over to remove the bars and cut for eating.

Pudding Pops

2 cups cold 2% milk
1 package (4-serving size) Jell-O
  instant pudding & pie filling,
  any flavor

Serves 6

Pour cold milk into medium bowl. Add pudding mix. Beat with wire whisk 2 minutes. Spoon into 6 (5-ounce) paper or plastic cups, then insert wooden pop stick or plastic spoon into each for a handle.

Freeze for 5 hours or until firm.

To remove pop from cup, place bottom of cup under warm running water for 15 seconds. Press firmly on bottom of cup to release pop. (Do not twist or pull pop stick).

Store leftover pops in freezer. Have fun and try several different flavors together.

Hannah in the kitchen – Chef Lou's daughter

Roasted Baby Potatoes

1 pound baby redskin potatoes
3 tablespoons olive oil
1 teaspoon dried rosemary
Salt and pepper to taste

Serves 4

Wash the potatoes, then cut in half or quarters. Drizzle with olive oil and seasonings.

Bake in a 350-degree oven until tender and golden brown, about 25 minutes.

Salmon in a Bag

4 (6-ounces) salmon fillets
3/4 cup leeks, washed, and
    julienne cut
3/4 cup zucchini squash,
    julienne cut
3/4 cup yellow squash,
    julienne cut
3/4 cup carrots, julienne cut
1 teaspoon dried thyme
1/2 teaspoon dried tarragon
2 tablespoons olive oil
4 tablespoons water
Juice of 1 lemon
1 teaspoon parsley, fresh chopped
1 teaspoon butter
4 pieces of parchment paper,
    cut into heart shapes
Salt and pepper to taste

Makes 4 portions

Preheat oven to 350 degrees. Fold parchment paper sheet in half and cut to form "heart," (14-inches top to bottom and 15-inches wide). Open parchment heart and place on work surface. Rub top side of heart lightly with butter.

Toss julienne vegetables together gently and place on one side of the paper. Lay one salmon fillet parallel to the crease on one side of the parchment heart on top of the vegetables.

Drizzle on the olive oil, water and lemon juice. Season with salt and pepper and the herbs. Fold remaining half of heart over to cover fish and begin to close making a series of small overlapping folds to seal, starting with the round end.

Continue until parchment pouch is completely sealed folding remaining tip under. Repeat process until all fish filets are wrapped.

Bake at 350 degrees for 8 to 10 minutes. Present in parchment bag, cutting open tableside.

Sparkling Fruity Jell-O Parfaits

1 cup boiling water
2 (3-ounce) packages Jell-O, flavor
   of your choice (we used peach)
3 cups cold club soda
1 cup strawberries, washed and
   sliced
1 cup watermelon balls or squares
1/2 cup blueberries, washed

Serves 8

In a large bowl, stir the boiling water into gelatin, stirring at least 2 minutes until completely dissolved. Stir in cold club soda. Refrigerate 1-1/2 hours or until set.

Use a fork to flake the Jell-O into small pieces. Spoon some Jell-O into a cup about a quarter of the way up. Add in some berries and melon. Add on more Jell-O.

Continue to layer until you reach almost to the top. Refrigerate 2 hours to firm. Garnish with whipped topping.

Summer Veggie Pizza

2 (8-ounce) packages refrigerated
   crescent rolls
16 ounces cream cheese, softened
1 cup mayonnaise
1 (1-ounce) package dry Ranch-
   style dressing mix
2 cups fresh broccoli, chopped
4 Roma tomatoes, thin wedges
1 green bell pepper, cut into rings
1 red bell pepper, cut into rings
1 cup cauliflower, chopped
1 cup carrot, shredded
2 cups shredded cheddar cheese

Serves 8

Preheat oven to 375 degrees. Roll out the crescent roll dough onto a 9x13-inch baking sheet and pinch together edges to form the pizza crust.

Bake crust for 12 minutes in the preheated oven. Once finished cooking, remove crust from oven and let cool 15 minutes without removing it from the baking sheet. Once removed, allow it to cool completely.

In a small mixing bowl, combine cream cheese, mayonnaise and dry Ranch dressing. Spread the mixture over the cooled crust. Arrange broccoli, tomato, peppers, cauliflower, shredded carrot, and cheddar cheese over the cream cheese layer. Chill for one hour, slice and serve.

Originally printed in the News-Leader, August 2007

Vanilla Ice Cream

2 cans sweetened condensed milk
3 cups heavy cream
2 cups whole milk
1 vanilla bean, split
2 tablespoons vanilla extract
1 cup sugar

Serves 6

Combine all ingredients until well mixed. Add to the ice cream maker and process until firm.

Breakfast

Apple Compote

2 medium Fuji or Granny Smith
  apples, peeled and diced
1/4 cup sugar
3/4 - 1 cup water
1 teaspoon cinnamon
1 teaspoon cornstarch
2 teaspoons lemon juice
Pinch of salt

Makes 2-1/2 cups

Add all the ingredients into a saucepan and stir over medium heat until the mixture comes to a boil.

Lower heat and simmer until the mixture becomes thick and the apples are soft. Feel free to add additional water as need to keep a sauce-like consistency.

Asparagus, Shrimp and Prosciutto Frittata

7 eggs
2/3 cup milk
1/3 cup plus 2 tablespoons
  parmesan cheese
2 tablespoons Dijon mustard
2 tablespoons olive oil
3 ounces prosciutto, sliced paper
  thin
1 small shallot
2 tablespoons onion, minced
1/3 pound thin asparagus,
  trimmed and sliced thin
1 cup cooked shrimp, chopped
Salt and pepper to taste

Makes 4 servings

Position an oven rack 4 to 6 inches from the broiler and turn the broiler on high.

In a bowl, whisk together the eggs, milk, 1/3 cup of the cheese, mustard, salt and pepper. Set aside.

Heat the oil in an 8-inch nonstick skillet over medium heat. Add the sliced prosciutto, shallot and asparagus and cook, stirring frequently, until the asparagus is crisp-tender.

Reduce the heat to low and pour the egg mixture and shrimp into the skillet. Stir to mix the ingredients then cook until the eggs are well set and slightly puffed around the edges but are still loose in the center, around 15 minutes.

Sprinkle the remaining 2 tablespoons of parmesan on top of the frittata. Slide the pan under the broiler and cook until browned and set, 3 to 4 minutes.

Let cool for 5 minutes then cut into wedges.

Originally printed in the News-Leader, March 2006

Blueberry Blintzes

3 eggs
8 ounces milk
1 ounce vegetable oil
3/4 teaspoon salt
4 ounces flour
12 ounces ricotta cheese
1 egg yolk
1/2 cup sugar
1 teaspoon lemon juice
1 teaspoon vanilla extract
2 ounces whole butter
1 1/2 cups blueberry pie filling

Serves 4

Whisk together the eggs, milk and oil. Add in half of the salt. Stir in the flour and mix until smooth.

Pour through a strainer to remove chunks and allow the batter to rest for 30 minutes.

Heat a 6-inch skillet to medium high and spray the pan with nonstick cooking spray.

Pour 2 ounces of the batter into the pan. Tip the pan so that the batter coats the entire surface in a thin layer. Cook the pancake until browned on the bottom.

Remove it from the pan, turn the crepe over and cook for about 30 seconds on the other side.

Repeat this procedure until all of the crepes are made.

To make the filling, drain the ricotta cheese in a colander, discarding the liquid. Place the drained cheese in a bowl with the egg yolk, sugar, the remaining salt, lemon juice and vanilla extract and mix well.

To assemble, place a pancake on the work surface with the browned side up. Place 1 ounce of the filling in the center of the pancake. Fold the opposite ends of the pancake in and then roll up to form a small package.

Sauté each blintz in butter until hot.

Top with blueberries and serve.

Breakfast Smoothie

1 (16-ounce) can frozen orange
    juice concentrate
1 pint heavy cream
1 cup vanilla yogurt
20 fluid ounces carbonated water
1/3 cup powdered sugar
2 1/2 teaspoons vanilla extract
15 cubes ice

Serves 6

In a blender, combine orange juice concentrate, cream, yogurt, carbonated water, powdered sugar, vanilla and ice. Blend until smooth.

Pour into glasses and serve immediately.

Breakfast Strudel

1 pound puff pastry
2 tablespoons unsalted butter
1 cup frozen cubed hash brown
    potatoes
1 cup red or green bell peppers,
    seeded, diced
1/2 cup onion, diced
1 cup artichokes
1 cup smoked ham, diced
11 eggs
4 ounces Monterey Jack cheese,
    shredded
2 tablespoons fresh chives,
    minced
1 egg
1 tablespoon water
2 tablespoons parmesan cheese,
    shredded

Makes 2 Strudels

Preheat oven to 400 degrees. Thaw pastry according to package directions, about 30 minutes.

Melt butter in a large nonstick skillet over medium-high heat. Add potatoes and sauté 5 minutes. Stir in bell pepper and onion; sauté 3 minutes, then add ham.

Whisk eggs and chives together. Add them to the pan and scramble just until set. Season with salt and pepper to taste; off heat, stir in cheese until blended and add the artichokes. Refrigerate this mixture while working with the pastry.

Unfold a pastry sheet on a work surface that's been lightly dusted with flour. Roll pastry lengthwise to 12x10 inches, then transfer to a piece of parchment cut to fit a baking sheet. Trim pastry; fill with the egg, potato and meat mixture. Egg wash the inside of the pastry and fold over the filling. Fold in the ends of the pastry and crimp to seal

Combine the remaining egg and water; brush over top of strudels. Cut a few slits in the top of the strudel for steam release.

Sprinkle with cheese and bake 20 to 30 minutes or until golden. Let cool 5 minutes for slicing.

Cinnamon Peach French Toast with Butter Pecan Syrup

10 eggs, beaten
4 ounces heavy cream
Salt to taste
Ground cinnamon to taste
12 slices thick cut bread such as
    sourdough, cinnamon, banana
    or brioche
1 cup peach preserves
Unsalted butter as needed
Powdered sugar as needed

Butter Pecan Syrup:
2 cups granulated sugar
1 cup water
1/3 cup dark corn syrup
4 tablespoons butter
2 teaspoons vanilla extract
1 teaspoon pumpkin pie spices
1/2 cup finely chopped pecans,
    toasted

Serves 4

Whisk together the eggs, cream, salt and cinnamon.

Place the egg mixture in a shallow pan. Place the slices of bread in the egg mixture and let soak for 2 to 3 minutes, turning them over after the first minute or so. Cook the slices of French toast on lightly buttered griddle.

Top with peach preserves and powdered sugar.

Butter Peach Syrup:
Add all ingredients together in a saucepan. Bring to a boil, reduce heat and simmer for an hour stirring as needed.

Cornmeal Pancakes

1/2 cup all-purpose flour
1/2 cup cornmeal
3 teaspoons baking powder
1/2 teaspoon salt
1 tablespoon sugar
1/2 cup boiling water
1/4 cup milk
1/4 cup corn oil
1 egg, beaten

Serves 2

Mix all ingredients in the order given.

In an ungreased heated skillet, drop batter one tablespoon at a time to make very small pancakes (about silver dollar size). Pancakes cook very quickly.

Eggs Benedict with Shrimp and Prosciutto with Choron Sauce

4 English muffins, split
Salt to taste
2 ounces vinegar
4 eggs
6 ounces hollandaise sauce
2 tablespoons tomato paste
4 slices thinly cut prosciutto
12 peeled and deveined shrimp
1 tablespoon butter

Makes 6 servings

Hollandaise Sauce:
4 egg yolks, pasteurized
2 ounces warm water
1 ounce lemon juice
Cayenne pepper to taste
1/2 teaspoon salt
1/4 teaspoon white pepper
Tabasco sauce to taste
12 ounces whole butter

Season the shrimp and sauté in a little butter until done. Slice in half lengthwise and set aside.

Toast the English muffin.

Bring 1 quart water to a boil and add the salt and vinegar. Add the eggs and poach until done. I like mine a little runny.

Place the muffins on a plate and top with the prosciutto slices and grilled shrimp. Place an egg on each slice of meat and cover with the choron sauce. Choron sauce is just hollandaise with a little tomato paste added in.

Hollandaise Sauce (blender method):
Place the egg yolks, water, lemon juice, cayenne pepper, salt, white pepper and Tabasco sauce in the bowl of the blender. Cover and blend on high speed for approximately 5 seconds.

Heat the butter to approximately 175 degrees. This allows the butter to cook the yolks as it is added to them.

Turn the blender on and immediately begin to add the butter in a steady stream. Incorporate all the butter in 20 to 30 seconds. Adjust the seasonings.

If any lumps are present, strain the sauce through a mesh strainer. Transfer the sauce to a bowl container and adjust the seasonings.

Fall Fruit Gratin

1 cup sliced apples
1 cup sliced pears
3/4 cup dried cranberries
1/2 cup toasted walnuts
1/4 teaspoon cinnamon
1 teaspoon lemon juice
1 teaspoon lemon zest
1/4 cup honey
1/2 cup white raisins
1 cup Panko bread crumbs
3 tablespoons butter, melted
1 tablespoon sugar
1 cup heavy cream
Pinch of salt

Makes 4 servings

Preheat oven to 375 degrees. Place raisins, cranberries, lemon juice and 1 cup of water in a small saucepan and bring to a simmer, uncovered. Allow to simmer till soft and plump, then drain.

Arrange sliced fruit in a gratin dish or other small oven-proof baking dish.

Scatter dried fruit over the sliced fruit and pour remaining liquid over the fruit as well.

Mix the cream with the honey and the salt. Pour over the fruit.

Mix the bread crumbs, sugar, the spices and the lemon rind together with the melted butter and scatter over the fruit.

Bake till fruit is bubbly (about 12 to 15 minutes).

Fruit and Almond Gratins

2 large eggs
1 cup heavy cream
1/2 cup brown sugar
1/2 teaspoon vanilla
1/8 teaspoon salt
2 cups berries of your choice
2 teaspoons fresh lemon juice
1 banana, cut up
1/2 cup seedless grapes, sliced
3/4 cup almonds, sliced
1/2 stick (1/4 cup) unsalted
   butter, cut into 1/2-inch cubes

Makes 4 servings

Butter the gratin dishes.

In a bowl combine the eggs, cream, brown sugar, vanilla, and salt and whisk together.

Toss fruit with lemon juice in a bowl, and then put in gratin dishes.

Pour custard mixture over fruit. Sprinkle with almonds and dot with butter.

Place the gratin dishes on a baking sheet and bake for 20 minutes in a 325-degree oven.

If desired, preheat your oven broiler to high and broil the gratins for a minute or two to brown the top.

German Pancake

5 ounces all-purpose flour
8 ounces milk
3 eggs
3 tablespoons sugar
1/4 teaspoon salt
1 teaspoon vanilla extract
1 tablespoon butter
Powdered sugar, as needed
Fresh juice, from 1/2 lemon
Jam or jelly for the topping

Serves 4

Place the flour in a large mixing bowl. In a separate container blend the milk, eggs, granulated sugar, salt and vanilla extract. Whisk the egg mixture into the flour, beating until well blended and smooth.

Place the butter in a heavy 10-inch skillet and put the skillet into a hot oven. When the pan is hot and the butter melted but not burned, remove the pan from the oven and immediately pour in the batter. Return the pan to a 425-degree oven and bake until puffed, dry and lightly browned, approximately 25 minutes.

Dust with powdered sugar, sprinkle with lemon juice and serve immediately with jam or jelly of your choice.

Huevos Rancheros

Vegetable oil, as needed
5 corn tortillas
10 eggs
8 ounces salsa
4 ounces Monterey Jack cheese
1 can chilies
Refried beans

Serves 5

Heat a thin layer of oil in a sauté pan. Fry the tortilla briefly in the oil, turning it once, until softened. Remove from the pan and drain on paper towels.

Fry the eggs sunny side up or basted. Place the tortilla on a warm dinner plate. Top with the eggs.

Ladle the salsa over the whites of the eggs, leaving the yolks uncovered. Top with the grated cheese. Serve with a side of beans, tomatoes and onion.

Mediterranean Mushroom and Roasted Red Pepper Quiche

2 ounces Swiss cheese, shredded
1 (10-inch) pie shell
2 cups mushrooms, sliced
1 cup roasted red pepper, sliced
4 eggs
1 pint milk
4 ounces heavy cream
Salt and pepper to taste
Nutmeg to taste

Serves 4

To make the custard, combine the eggs, milk and cream. Season with salt, pepper and nutmeg and mix well.

Pour the custard over the mushrooms, red peppers and cheese in the pie shell and bake at 350 degrees until the custard is set and it reaches an internal temperature of 160 degrees, approximately 1 hour.

Mexicali McMuffin

4 slices Pepper Jack cheese
6 ounces chorizo sausage
4 poached eggs
2 English muffin halves
1 cup hollandaise sauce
  (see page 134)
1/2 cup salsa

Serves 4

Cook the chorizo. Toast muffins.

Mix a little salsa with hollandaise.

Place a poached egg on a muffin top with chorizo and cheese then another muffin half. Serve the salsa hollandaise on the side.

My Tex Mex Scrambled Eggs

8 (6-inch) corn tortillas
Vegetable oil
8 large eggs
1/4 cup milk
1/4 cup salsa
Dash of hot sauce
1/2 teaspoon garlic powder
Salt and black pepper
1 tablespoon olive oil
1/2 cup Monterey Jack cheese,
  grated

Makes 4 servings

Garnish:
Sour cream
Salsa
Black olives
Jalapeno pepper rings
Green onions

Heat oil in pan and fry the tortillas until crisp, then set aside and drain.

Combine the eggs, milk, salsa, hot sauce, salt to taste and pepper. Whisk until blended.

Heat the oil in large nonstick skillet over medium heat. Add eggs and cook, stirring gently until soft-set, 3 to 5 minutes.

Sprinkle eggs with cheese.

Spoon eggs onto the tortillas and garnish with the choices at left.

Originally printed in the News-Leader, April 2007

Puffy Sweet Omelet

6 eggs, separated
1 teaspoon salt
2 tablespoons sugar
2 tablespoons butter
Fruit preserves of your choice
Powdered sugar

Serves 2

Heat oven to 325 degrees. In large bowl, combine egg whites and salt; beat until stiff peaks form. Set aside. With same beaters, in small bowl beat egg yolks and sugar until thickened and light yellow in color. Fold into egg whites.

Melt butter in 10-inch ovenproof skillet over medium heat; tilt pan to coat. Pour in egg mixture. Reduce heat to low; cook about 5 minutes or until puffy and light brown on bottom.

Place skillet in oven. Bake at 325 degrees for 15 to 18 minutes or until knife inserted in center comes out clean.

To remove from pan, tip skillet, loosening omelet with pancake turner. Spoon on preserves and fold in half. Slip onto platter and dust with sugar.

Originally printed in the News-Leader, March 2006

Simple Shirred Eggs

Butter, melted, as needed
1/2 ounce baked ham, sliced thin
2 eggs
Salt and pepper to taste
1 tablespoon heavy cream, hot
1 tablespoon Swiss cheese, grated

Makes 2 servings

Brush the interior of a 6-ounce ramekin with melted butter. Place the ham in the ramekin. Add in the cheese.

Break the eggs into a cup and pour them carefully into the ramekin on top of the ham.

Season with salt and pepper.

Pour on the cream, then bake at 325 degrees until the eggs begin to set, 8 to 10 minutes.

Feel free to add any combination of cheeses, meats or vegetables.

Originally printed in the News-Leader, February 2005

Stuffed Eggs Florentine

3/4 cup minced mushrooms
2 1/2 tablespoons butter
6 hard cooked eggs, halved
1 cup Mornay sauce
1 cup frozen spinach, chopped,
   drained
Salt to taste
1 tablespoon grated parmesan
   cheese

Mornay Sauce:
3 egg yolks
1/2 cup heavy cream
2 cups hot Béchamel
   (a white sauce)
2 tablespoons butter
2 tablespoons grated Gruyere
   (a style of Swiss cheese)

Serves 3

Preheat the broiler. In a small skillet, sauté the mushrooms in 1 tablespoon butter until the liquid evaporates.

Remove the yolks from the eggs and force through a sieve. Mix the yolks with the remaining butter, mushrooms, 1/4 cup Mornay sauce, spinach and salt. Fit a pastry bag with #4 plain tip and stuff the eggs.

Place a thin layer of Mornay sauce in the bottom of a baking dish and arrange the eggs on top. Coat each egg with the remaining sauce and sprinkle with the cheese. Brown under the broiler.

Can be prepared the day before and reheated at 350 degrees until bubbling hot. Brown the top under the broiler if necessary. (Can also be prepared ahead and frozen).

Mornay Sauce:
In a small bowl, mix the egg yolks and cream. In a small saucepan, heat the Béchamel. Cook, stirring constantly, until the sauce just reaches the boiling point. Stir in the cheese and swirl in the butter just before using. Heat only enough to melt the cheese.

The Perfect Home Pancakes

2 cups cake flour
4 tablespoons sugar
2 tablespoons baking powder
1/2 teaspoon salt
2 large eggs, slightly beaten
4 tablespoons melted butter
Milk, to make batter easy to pour

Makes 2-4 servings

Combine all of the dry ingredients and mix well. Stir in the beaten egg, melted butter and enough milk to make sure the batter is thin enough to pour. Mix lightly to blend.

Grease a flat-top griddle well and bring to medium-high heat.

Pour a half cup of batter onto the griddle and cook pancakes until bubbles start to form on top. Turn over and cook for another 60 seconds

Originally printed in the News-Leader, February 2005

Whatever Frittata

2 ounces chicken breast meat, boneless, skinless
1 teaspoon chopped garlic
Ground cumin to taste
Salt and pepper to taste
1 ounce mushrooms, sliced
1/2 fluid ounce unsalted butter
1 teaspoon jalapeno, seeded, minced
1 ounce red bell pepper, roasted, peeled, seeded, julienned
1 ounce green onions, sliced
3 eggs beaten
1 ounce Monterey Jack or cheddar cheese, shredded

Serves 2

Rub the chicken breast with the garlic, cumin, salt and pepper. Grill or broil the chicken until done. Allow it to rest briefly and then cut it into strips.

In a well-seasoned 9-inch sauté pan, sauté the mushrooms in the butter until tender. Add the jalapeno and sauté for 30 seconds. Add the chicken, bell pepper, green onions and cilantro and sauté until hot.

Add the eggs and season with salt and pepper. Cook the mixture, stirring and lifting the eggs to help them cook evenly, until they begin to set.

Sprinkle the cheese over the eggs and place under a salamander or broiler to melt the cheese and finish cooking the eggs. Slide the frittata onto a plate or cut into wedges for smaller portions.

Breads, Pastas & Grains

Basic Cornbread

1 cup yellow cornmeal
1/3 cup flour
1/4 teaspoon baking soda
1 teaspoon baking powder
1 teaspoon salt
1 egg, beaten
1 cup buttermilk
3 tablespoons sugar
1/4 cup bacon grease for pan

Serves 8

Combine dry ingredients; add beaten egg and buttermilk, mixing well.

Pour into greased, heated 9-inch iron skillet.

Bake at 400 degrees for 20 minutes or until lightly browned.

Originally printed in the News-Leader, November 2006

Basic Pie Dough (flaky)

2 1/2 cups flour
1 teaspoon salt
1 cup unsalted butter (chilled)
1/4 – 1/2 cup ice water

Makes 1 dough

Combine the salt and flour.

Using your hands or forks, cut or mix the butter into the flour until the butter and flour look like small peas.

Add in ice water and mix until just combined.

Wrap in plastic wrap and let sit in the cooler for 2 to 3 hours.

Roll out and use as needed

Originally printed in the News-Leader, October 2003

Basic Pie Dough (mealy)

2 1/2 cups flour
1 teaspoon salt
3/4 cup unsalted butter
  (chilled)
1/4 cup ice water

Makes 1 dough

Follow the same procedure as above but:
Change the water to 1/4 cup only.
Decrease the unsalted butter to 3/4 cup.
Combine the fat and flour to resemble coarse cornmeal.

Originally printed in the News-Leader, October 2003

Cornbread - Tex Mex Style

1 1/2 cups cornmeal
1 teaspoon salt
1 teaspoon baking soda
1 1/2 cups buttermilk
1 egg, lightly beaten
2 tablespoons melted butter
1/4 cup Anaheim chili peppers,
  chopped
Jalapeno chili peppers, chopped
1 cup cream-style corn
1 cup cheddar cheese, shredded

Serves 6

Preheat the oven to 400 degrees.
In mixing bowl, combine cornmeal, salt and baking soda. Add buttermilk and egg; beat until batter is smooth. Add in the remaining ingredients and mix well.

Place butter in 8-inch square pan, baking dish or cast iron pan and heat in preheated oven.

Pour batter into the heated pan and bake for 35 minutes.

Originally printed in the News-Leader, November 2006

Corny Corn Bread

1/2 cup vegetable oil
1/4 cup oil for greasing pan
1 cup self-rising cornmeal
3/4 cup self-rising flour
1 cup cream-style corn
2 eggs
1 cup sour cream
3 tablespoons honey
Pinch of black pepper

Makes 8 Servings

Preheat oven to 375 degrees.
Generously season a cast iron skillet with up to 1/4 cup vegetable oil. Preheat the pan either in the oven or on the stove over medium-high heat.

Mix all ingredients together in a large bowl, stirring with a rubber spatula until combined.

Pour batter into the preheated cast iron skillet. Place skillet in the oven and bake until golden brown, approximately 30 minutes.

Dried Cherry Couscous

1 package couscous
  (10-ounce size)
1/3 cup olive oil
1 large carrot, diced fine
1 red bell pepper, diced fine
1 yellow bell pepper, diced fine
1 cup green onions, chopped
1 cup sour cherries, diced

Serves 4

Prepare the couscous according to package directions, substituting chicken broth or stock for the water. In the olive oil, sauté the carrot and pepper for about 3 minutes.

Toss with the cooked couscous, cherries, salt and pepper. Garnish with green onions. Then serve with chicken, duck or pork.

Easy Leavened Pita Bread

2 cups warm water
1 teaspoon sugar
1 package dry yeast
5 cups all-purpose flour
1/4 cup vegetable oil
2 teaspoons salt

Makes 16 pitas

In a mixing bowl, combine water and sugar; sprinkle yeast and let stand for 10 minutes. Using an electric mixer, beat in 2 cups of the flour, oil and salt; beat for about 3 minutes or until smooth, scraping down side of bowl from time to time.

With wooden spoon, beat in enough of the remaining flour to make stiff dough. Turn out onto lightly floured surface and knead for about 10 minutes or until smooth and elastic. Place dough in lightly greased bowl, turning to grease all over. Cover with plastic wrap and let rise for 1 to 1-1/2 hours or until doubled in bulk.

Divide dough into 16 pieces. On lightly floured surface, roll each piece into 7-inch rounds. Cover and let rise for 15 minutes.

Heat an ungreased baking sheet on lowest rack in a 500-degree oven. Using floured metal spatula, quickly transfer pita rounds to heated baking sheet; bake for 3 or 4 minutes or until puffed and light golden around edges.

Repeat with remaining pita rounds.

Let cool between damp tea towels. Pitas will collapse and soften slightly, but pocket will remain.

Originally printed in the News-Leader, February 2005

Easy Blackberry Yogurt Muffins

1 cup blackberries
2 tablespoons sugar
1 large egg
1 cup vanilla yogurt
3 tablespoons butter, melted
2 1/2 cups Bisquick
1 teaspoon chopped lemon zest

Makes 12 muffins

Preheat oven to 400 degrees.
Sprinkle berries with sugar; toss lightly to coat; set aside.

In a large bowl, beat egg; add yogurt and melted butter. Beat until smooth, then add in the Bisquick and stir until just blended.

Gently fold in the berries and lemon zest.

Spoon the batter into regular size, greased muffin cups. Fill about halfway to three-fourths full.

Bake for 20 to 25 minutes, or until a toothpick inserted in the center comes out clean.

Cool for 5 minutes in cups, then finish cooling on rack.

Eggless Apple Muffins

2 cups flour
1/2 cup sugar
2 1/2 teaspoons baking powder
1 teaspoon cinnamon
1/2 teaspoon salt
2 medium Granny Smith apples
1/2 cup vegetable oil
1/2 cup sour cream
3/4 cup applesauce
1 tablespoon sugar

Makes 12 muffins

Preheat oven to 400 degrees.
Combine flour, 1/2 cup sugar, baking powder, cinnamon and salt together and set aside.

Peel, core and dice apples into small bits. In a medium bowl combine oil, sour cream and apple sauce. Add dry ingredients and apples and stir to combine. Batter will be stiff so do not overwork. Divide batter between 12 greased muffin tins. Sprinkle remaining 1 tablespoon sugar over muffins.

Bake at 400 degrees for 18 to 20 minutes or until a toothpick inserted in the middle comes out clean. Let the muffins sit in the pans for 2 minutes before removing to a cooling rack.

Originally printed in the News-Leader, November 2006

Fettuccine Alfredo with Morels

1 stick (1/2 cup) unsalted butter
1 cup heavy cream
2 tablespoons brandy
1 1/4 pounds fresh morels, rinsed, drained, and cut into rings
1 pound fettuccine
1 tablespoon fresh lemon juice
3/4 cup parmesan cheese, grated
4 tablespoons parmesan, grated for sprinkling on top
1 tablespoon chives, minced for garnish

Serves 4

In a skillet melt 2 tablespoons of the butter over moderately low heat, add the cream, the brandy, and salt and pepper to taste, and bring the mixture to a boil. Add the morels, simmer them, covered, for 10 minutes, and keep the mixture warm.

In a kettle of boiling salted water cook the fettuccine until it is al dente. While the pasta is cooking, in a large deep skillet melt the remaining 6 tablespoons butter over low heat. Drain the pasta, add it to the large skillet, and toss it with the butter.

Add the morel mixture, 1/2 cup of the parmesan, lemon juice, salt and pepper to taste and toss the mixture well.

Garnish with the chives and remaining parmesan cheese. Substitute any mushrooms if morels are not available.

Originally printed in the News-Leader, April 2004

Fruity Rice Pilaf

2 tablespoons butter
1 tablespoon olive oil
1 onion, finely chopped
2 garlic cloves, crushed
1 red bell pepper, seeded and diced
1 1/4 cups long grain rice
1 teaspoon ground coriander
2 teaspoons ground cumin
2 tablespoons honey
2/3 cup golden raisins
2/3 cup dried apricots, chopped
3 cups chicken stock
1/2 teaspoon red pepper flakes
Salt and ground pepper
3/4 cup pistachios or almonds

Serves 4

Melt butter with olive oil in large skillet over medium heat; add rice, onion, bell pepper, pepper flakes and garlic. Cook, stirring constantly, for 3 to 4 minutes or until rice is golden brown.

Add chicken stock, apricots, raisins, honey, spice and seasonings.

Bring mixture to a boil. Reduce heat to low; cover. Cook, stirring occasionally, for 20 to 25 minutes or until rice is tender and most of liquid is absorbed. Stir in crushed nuts and serve.

Originally printed in the News-Leader, April 2006

Herbed Corn Bread

1 1/2 cups flour
2 tablespoons sugar
4 teaspoons baking powder
2 teaspoons salt
1 teaspoon sage
1 teaspoon dried thyme
1 1/2 cups cornmeal
1 tablespoon onion powder
1/4 cup pimientos, chopped and
  drained
3 eggs, beaten
1 1/2 cups milk
1/3 cup vegetable oil

Serves 6

In a large bowl, combine the flour, sugar, baking powder, salt, sage and thyme.

Combine cornmeal, celery, onion and pimientos; add to dry ingredients and mix well.

Add eggs, milk and oil; stir just until moistened.

Pour into a greased 10-inch ovenproof skillet.

Bake at 400 degrees for 35 to 45 minutes or until bread tests done.

Mushroom Risotto

4 tablespoons butter
2 cups crimini or button
  mushrooms, cleaned and diced
1/3 cup white wine
3/4 cup heavy cream
7 cups chicken stock
1 tablespoon olive oil
1 onion, peeled and minced
1 3/4 cups Arborio rice
1/3 cup parmesan cheese, grated
Salt and pepper to taste

Serves 4-6.

Sauté mushrooms and onions in a skillet with 2 tablespoons of butter for 5 minutes.

Add white wine, bring to a boil, and reduce the liquid until it is almost gone. Stir in the rice.

Add stock, 1/2 cup at a time. When the stock is almost absorbed add the next 1/2 cup. This process will take about 20 minutes.

The rice should be just cooked and slightly chewy. Stir in remaining butter, cream and the parmesan cheese. Season to taste.

Originally printed in the News-Leader, March 2006

Nutty Banana Bread with Chocolate Peanut Butter Spread

4 very over ripe bananas
1 cup sugar
1 2/3 cups all-purpose flour
1/3 cup oat flour
1 teaspoon baking soda
1 teaspoon salt
8 tablespoons melted butter
2 large eggs
2 teaspoons almond extract
1 cup pecans, chopped

Makes 1 loaf or about 8 servings

Chocolate Peanut Butter Spread:
1/2 cup semi-sweet chocolate
  chips
1 1/2 cups smooth peanut butter
1/4 cup butter (softened)
1/4 cup powdered sugar
1 teaspoon vanilla extract
1 teaspoon instant coffee
  granules
1 teaspoon hot water

Yield: about 2 cups

Preheat oven to 350 degrees.
Grease a loaf pan with vegetable shortening and line it with wax or parchment paper. Mash bananas together with sugar until smooth.

Mix together all of the dry ingredients: flours, soda and salt. Whisk together the moist ingredients and add to the dry. Fold in the nuts.

Bake for 50 minutes to 1 hour on the middle rack of the oven. A toothpick inserted in the middle should come out clean.

Let the bread cool for 15 minutes in the pan, then remove to finish cooling.

Chocolate Peanut Butter Spread:
Melt chocolate chips in a double-boiler or in the microwave until smooth, taking care not to scorch the chocolate.

Allow the chocolate to cool slightly then mix it into the peanut butter, butter, sugar and vanilla extract. Stir until thoroughly combined.

Mix instant coffee with hot water until completely dissolved. Add coffee to the chocolate peanut butter mixture until combined.

Originally printed in the News-Leader, June 2006

Nutty Brown Rice Pilaf

1 teaspoon vegetable oil
1 onion, chopped
2 cloves garlic, minced
1 teaspoon thyme
Pinch cinnamon
1 cup long grain brown rice
2 cups chicken stock
1/3 cup dried cranberries
1 teaspoon grated lemon rind
1/2 cup pecans, toasted
1/4 cup pine nuts, toasted
2 green onions diced
Salt and pepper to taste

Serves 4 as a side or
   2 as an entree

In a saucepan, heat oil over medium heat; cook onion, garlic, thyme, salt, pepper and cinnamon, stirring often, for 5 minutes.

Add rice; cook, stirring, for 1 minute. Add stock, cranberries and lemon rind; bring to boil. Reduce heat to low; cover and cook for 45 minutes or until rice is tender and liquid is absorbed.

Add in the pecans Let stand, covered, for 5 minutes; fluff with fork.

Sprinkle with pine nuts and onions.

Pasta with Lemon Chicken Oregano and Feta

4 boneless, skinless chicken breast
   halves
3 tablespoons olive oil
3/4 teaspoon lemon pepper
   seasoning
1/4 cup fresh oregano, chopped or
   2 teaspoons dried oregano
Juice of 1/2 lemon
3/4 cup chicken broth
4 tablespoons feta cheese,
   crumbled
8 ounces linguine pasta, cooked
   and tossed with a little extra
   virgin olive oil
Salt and pepper to taste

Serves 4

Heat large skillet; add olive oil. Season both sides of chicken breasts with lemon pepper and half of oregano. Add chicken; brown on one side approximately 3 minutes.

While chicken is cooking, combine lemon juice, broth and remainder of oregano.

Turn chicken and brown the other side. Add broth mixture and cook 6 minutes or until the chicken juices run clear.

Cut the chicken into pieces and toss with the pasta and the remaining pan juices.

Toss well, then sprinkle on the feta cheese.

Originally printed in the News-Leader, February 2005

Penne with Gorgonzola and Walnuts

2 tablespoons butter
1/2 cup onion, finely chopped
1 tablespoon dried thyme
2 cups whipping cream
6 ounces Gorgonzola cheese,
  crumbled
1 1/2 pound penne pasta
1 cup walnuts, coarsely chopped
  and slightly toasted
1/2 cup Romano cheese
Salt and pepper to taste

Serves 4

Melt butter in heavy medium skillet. Add onion and sauté until translucent, about 5 minutes. Stir in thyme. Add cream and Gorgonzola and stir until cheese melts and sauce thickens slightly. Season with salt and pepper.

Cook pasta in large pot of rapidly boiling salted water until firm to the bite. Drain pasta well and return to the pot.

Add sauce and stir over low heat until pasta is coated. Mix in walnuts. Put in a serving dish and sprinkle with Romano cheese and a few reserved walnuts.

Originally printed in the News-Leader, October 2006

Pita Bread (unleavened and thin)

3 cups white flour
1 teaspoon salt
1 cup warm water
Vegetable oil

Makes 12 pitas

Combine the flour and salt; stir in enough warm water so that the dough pulls away from the sides of the bowl and is no longer sticky. Stir till smooth. Knead for 5 minutes.

Shape dough into rectangle and cut in half lengthwise. Divide into 12 portions and shape into smooth balls. Cover with damp cloth and let rest 5 to 10 minutes.

Press each ball flat and roll into a 6- or 7-inch circle. Cover with damp towels.

Lightly oil a griddle or skillet. Gently stretch each round as thin as possible.

Cook until brown and bubbly spots appear on the bottom, about 90 seconds. Turn over and brown the other side.

Remove from griddle and wrap immediately in towels.

Originally printed in the News-Leader, Febraury 2005

Roasted Onion and Olive Focaccia

12 ounces all-purpose flour
(plus a little for dusting)
1/2 teaspoon salt
1 1/2 tablespoons extra virgin
olive oil
8 ounces warm water

Topping:
2 small red onions cut into thin
slices
5 ounces pitted sliced black olives
1 tablespoon kosher salt
2 tablespoons extra virgin olive
oil

Makes 6 servings

Sift the flour and salt into a large mixing bowl, then sprinkle in the yeast and stir.

Pour in water along with olive oil and mix everything into a dough that leaves the sides of the bowl clean.

Turn the dough out onto a lightly floured surface and knead it for about 10 minutes or use an electric mixer with a dough hook and process for 5 minutes.

When the dough feels bouncy and elastic, return it to the bowl. Cover with plastic wrap and leave in a warm place until it has doubled in size, about 1-1/2 hours or more depending on the heat in the kitchen.

When risen, turn the dough out on to the work surface and punch the air out by kneading it again for 2 to 3 minutes.

Take two-thirds of the olives and push them into the dough.

Pat the dough into an oblong loaf, rounded at the ends. Sprinkle on the remaining olives and onions.

Drizzle the olive oil all over the top and lightly salt with the kosher salt.

Cover with a damp cloth and let the dough puff up again for 30 minutes.

Preheat the oven to 450 degrees. Bake the bread for about 15 to 20 minutes or until golden around the edges and well cooked in the center. Cool on a wire rack

When cool, top with your favorite version of tuna salad for a great sandwich.

Originally printed in the News-Leader, June 2004

Sweet Potato Walnut Bread

1/2 cup butter
1/2 cup shortening
2 2/3 cups sucanat
4 eggs
2 cups cold, mashed sweet
  potatoes
3 1/2 cups flour
1 teaspoon salt
1 teaspoon cinnamon
2 teaspoons nutmeg
2 teaspoons baking soda
1 cup walnuts, toasted and
  chopped
1/3 cup cold strong black coffee
1/3 cup orange juice

Makes 3 loaves

Cream together butter shortening and sucanat. Add eggs one at a time, blending well after each addition. Blend in sweet potatoes.

Mix together dry ingredients and nuts. Stir into creamed mixture alternately with coffee and orange juice.

Pour batter into 3 greased loaf pans and bake at 375 degrees for 1 hour or until a toothpick inserted into the middle of the bread comes out clean.

Cool 10 minutes; remove from pans and cool completely.

Tabbouleh or Mediterranean Parsley and Wheat Salad

1 cup medium bulgur
2 cups boiling water
4 large ripe tomatoes,
  finely chopped
1 cup chopped parsley sprigs
1 cup peeled and chopped
  cucumber
1/4 cup packed mint sprigs,
  chopped
1 bunch scallions, finely chopped
1 medium onion, finely chopped
1/2 teaspoon garlic powder
1 teaspoon salt
1/2 teaspoon black pepper
1/2 cup fresh lemon juice
1/3 cup extra virgin olive oil

Serves 4

Cover the bulgur with the boiling water and let stand for 30 minutes or until tender. The bulgur will remain a little chewy but not overly tough.

Drain very well, pressing the bulgur down with a spoon to get rid of the extra water.

Place the bulgur a bowl and add in all of the remaining ingredients except for the lemon juice and oil. Mix together well.

Stir the lemon juice and oil together and add to the other ingredients.

Feel free to add additional lemon juice and seasonings to meet your personal tastes. You can also crumble about one cup of feta cheese on top to make this more of a meal.

Originally printed in the News-Leader, May 2007

Miscellaneous

Basic Blend for Fish or Chicken

1 tablespoon dried basil
2 teaspoons dried tarragon
2 tablespoons dried thyme
1 teaspoon dried oregano
1 bay leaf

Makes 1/2 cup

Combine all of the ingredients in a food processor or blender. Use this dry rub when grilling or saut ing.

Originally printed in the News-Leader, March 2005

Basic Meat Marinade

2 tablespoons Worcestershire
 sauce
1/2 cup oil
2 teaspoons salt
1/4 cup vinegar
2 teaspoons parsley
2 tablespoons soy sauce
1 tablespoon mustard
2 teaspoons pepper
1/4 cup red wine vinegar
2 teaspoons garlic powder

Makes 1 1/2 cups

Combine all of the ingredients in a zip seal bag and shake well.

Add the meat and marinate overnight.

Use this for grilled beef or chicken.

Originally printed in the News-Leader, September 2005

Basic Spice Rub for Beef or Pork

4 tablespoons dried rosemary
 leaves
4 tablespoons dried thyme
2 tablespoons onion powder
1 tablespoon garlic powder
2 teaspoons coarse kosher salt
1/2 teaspoon ground black pepper

Makes about 1 cup

Combine all of the ingredients in a food processor or blender.

Originally printed in the News-Leader, March 2005

Blackberry Cabernet Sauce

2 cups blackberries
3 tablespoons extra virgin olive
    oil
1 small onion, chopped
3 tablespoons sugar
1 cup Cabernet Sauvignon wine

Makes about 2 cups

In a food processor or blender, puree and then strain enough blackberries to measure 1 cup pulp.

In a large frying pan, sauté onion in olive oil approximately 5 minutes or until onions are transparent.

Add the blackberry pulp, sugar and wine. Simmer sauce until reduced to approximately half the original quantity. Remove from heat and let cool. Refrigerate until ready to use.

This sauce is good with turkey, duck or pork.

Originally printed in the News-Leader, June 2005

Blue Cheese Ranch Dipping Sauce

2 cups mayonnaise
1 cup sour cream
1/2 cup buttermilk
5 ounces blue cheese crumbles
2 tablespoons green onions, minced
1 teaspoon garlic, minced

Makes 4 cups

Whisk all ingredients together and let chill until ready to use. This may be thinned out with a little extra buttermilk.

Originally printed in the News-Leader, January 2007

Candied Lemon Peel

Lemon rind from 2 lemons
2 cups sugar
2 cups water

Makes 3/4 cup

Scrub the outside of the lemon rinds thoroughly to remove any dirt. Mix sugar and water until the sugar is dissolved over medium heat and bring to a simmer.

Scrape away the pithy white part of the peel. Slice into strips. Put rind in syrup and cook slowly until syrup is completely absorbed - several hours.

Cool the peel and coat the strips with granulated sugar. Dry overnight on a rack.

Caramelized Onion Relish

2 tablespoons olive oil
4 cups (about 3 medium) thinly
    sliced onions (1/8-inch thick)
3 cloves garlic, minced
1/2 teaspoon salt
1/4 teaspoon pepper
1 tablespoon packed brown sugar
1 tablespoon balsamic vinegar
1 teaspoon mustard seed

Makes 1 cup

Heat oil in large nonstick skillet over medium heat until hot. Add onions, garlic, salt and pepper; cook 30 minutes, stirring occasionally. Stir in brown sugar and vinegar; cook and stir until liquid has evaporated.

Cool for service.

Originally printed in the News-Leader, March 2005

Cilantro Chutney

1 cup cilantro leaves and stems,
    tightly packed
1 cup grated coconut
2 hot green chilies, seeded
2 tablespoons lime juice
1/2 teaspoon salt
1 teaspoon sugar
1 teaspoon ground ginger
1 garlic clove
1 cup water

Makes about 3 cups

Put all the ingredients except the water in a blender or food processor. Add water a little at a time and blend.

Scrape down the sides and keep adding water and blending until the mixture is a thick paste. The goal is to use just enough water to make a thick sauce consistency.

Originally printed in the News-Leader, June 2004

Corn Sauce

2 tablespoons butter
2 ears corn, scraped clean
1/4 cup chopped onions
1/4 cup chopped green onions
1 tablespoon minced garlic
2 cups chicken stock
1 tablespoon honey
1 tablespoon butter
Salt and pepper to taste

Makes 2 cups

Heat a medium skillet over high heat. Add the butter, corn, salt and pepper and cook, shaking the skillet from time to time to char the corn evenly, for about 2 minutes. Add the onions, green onions, honey and garlic and cook for 5 minutes or until tender.

Add the stock and bring to a boil. Reduce the heat and simmer for 15 minutes. Remove from the heat. Purée in a blender until smooth and then strain. Add in a pat of butter for richness, then serve.

Serve with roast pork or chicken.

Corn Salsa

2 cups fresh corn, blanched in
  boiling water
1/2 cup green pepper, chopped
1/4 cup red bell pepper, chopped
1/2 cup red onion, chopped
1 tomato, chopped
1/4 cup green onions, minced
2 tablespoons jalapeno peppers,
  chopped
1 teaspoon pickled jalapeno
  pepper juice
2 tablespoons lime juice
1 tablespoon olive oil
1/2 teaspoon garlic powder
1/2 teaspoon pepper
2 tablespoons olive oil
Salt and pepper to taste

Makes 5 cups

Combine all the corn salsa ingredients in a large bowl.

Cover the corn salsa and chill for several hours.

Adjust the seasonings before serving.

Cranberry Curd

1 (12-ounces) package fresh
  cranberries
2/3 cup water
Juice of one lemon
2 teaspoons cornstarch
1 cup sugar
4 egg yolks
6 tablespoons unsalted butter

Makes about 5 cups

Bring the cranberries to a boil in a medium saucepan over medium heat along with the water, lemon juice, cornstarch and sugar. Cook for 5 minutes or so, stirring and mashing until pulpy and all the berries have popped. If necessary, add a tablespoon or two more of water.

Remove from the heat and press the mixture through a coarse sieve so that you have a smooth puree.

Let cool slightly, then poor the puree back into the pot and beat in the egg yolks. Cook over medium-low heat for another 3 to 4 minutes until the curd thickens a bit (but don t let it boil). Remove from heat and pour into a bowl.

Whisk in the butter, 1 tablespoon at a time, until smooth. Cover with plastic, pressing right down on the surface to prevent a skin from forming, and let cool completely.

Fresh Watermelon Salsa

1/4 cup fresh lime juice
2 tablespoons golden brown
  sugar, packed
3 cups seeded watermelon,
  chopped
1 cup seeded cantaloupe,
  chopped
1 medium cucumber, peeled,
  seeded and chopped
1/2 cup red onion, chopped
1/4 cup fresh mint, chopped
2 tablespoons crystallized ginger,
  minced
2 tablespoons seeded jalapeno
  peppers, minced
Salt and pepper to taste

Makes 6 cups

Whisk lime juice and sugar in a large bowl until sugar dissolves.

Add watermelon and all remaining ingredients; toss gently.

Season with salt and pepper.

Originally printed in the News-Leader, September 2004

Homemade Basic Indian Curry Powder

4 dried red chilies
  (cayenne peppers)
1 ounce ground coriander seeds
2 tablespoons ground turmeric
1 tablespoon ground cumin
1 teaspoon mustard seeds
1 teaspoon black peppercorns
1 teaspoon fenugreek seeds
1 teaspoon ground ginger

Makes 1/2 cup

Combine all ingredients in a mortar and pestle or a food processor and grind into a fine powder.

Store in an airtight container for no longer than six months.

Originally printed in the News-Leader, March 2006

Homemade Crème Fraiche

1 cup whipping cream
2 tablespoons buttermilk

Makes about 1-1/2 cups

Combine the whipping cream and buttermilk in a non-reactive pan and over medium heat slowly bring up to about 100 degrees. Pour the mixture into a sterilized glass jar, like a mayonnaise jar.

Let the mixture sit in the jar for about 24 hours in a slightly high room temperature area. Maybe by the stove or light bulb from a lamp. The mixture will thicken as it sits.

Line a strainer with rinsed cheesecloth, a wet napkin or a coffee filter and fill it with the crème frâiche. Place the strainer over a bowl and refrigerate. Let strain for about 8 hours.

Originally printed in the News-Leader, June 2006

Horseradish Apricot Dipping Sauce

1 cup apricot preserves
6 tablespoons prepared horseradish

Makes 1-1/2 cups

Combine the ingredients and use as a dip for fried food.

Originally printed in the News-Leader, October 2006

Lemon Caper Supreme Sauce

Step 1:
2 ounces flour
2 ounces butter
1 quart chicken stock

Step 2:
2 tablespoons onion, minced
1/2 cup mushrooms, chopped
1 pint chicken sauce from Step 1
4 ounces heavy cream
1/2 ounce butter
4 tablespoons lemon juice, or to taste
4 tablespoons capers

Makes 1-1/2 pints

Melt the butter in a saucepan. Add in the flour all at once and stir to cook. Stir over medium heat for about 3 minutes. Put the roux into another pan and cool to use.

TIP: Add cold roux to hot stock or hot roux to cold liquid for proper thickening. Beat the cold roux into the hot stock. Bring to a boil and then reduce to a simmer, stirring frequently. Add in the onion and mushroom.

Simmer very slowly for an hour. Stir occasionally and skim the surface as necessary. Reduce the sauce by one-fourth, then add in the cream. Season with the lemon juice. Strain the sauce to remove the bits of onion and mushroom and return to the heat. Finish the sauce by stirring in the butter and capers. Serve immediately

Orange Curd

6 tablespoons softened unsalted
  butter
1 cup sugar
2 large eggs
2 large egg yolks
2 tablespoons lemon juice
1 cup orange juice
1 tablespoon orange zest

Serves 4

Orange curd can be used as a desert sauce or as a topper for biscuits and scones. In a large bowl, cream butter and sugar together with an electric mixer until a paste is formed. Add 1 egg at a time while mixing and then add yolks one at a time. Beat for 1 minute. Mix in the lemon and orange juice.

In a saucepan, cook the mixture over low heat until the white butter/sugar particles dissolve, stirring constantly. Increase to medium heat and cook for about 10 to 15 minutes until the mixture reaches 170 degrees on a candy thermometer or thickens enough to coat the back of a spoon. Do not let mixture boil. Remove curd from heat. Stir in orange zest. Pour curd into a medium-sized bowl and cover the surface with plastic wrap. Chill curd in refrigerator (it will thicken further as it chills).

Sweet and Tangy BBQ Sauce

2 tablespoons butter
1 small onion, minced
2 cups ketchup
1/2 cup cider vinegar
1/4 cup apple juice
1/4 cup Worcestershire sauce
3 tablespoons brown sugar
2 tablespoons molasses
2 tablespoons honey
2 teaspoons dry mustard
1 teaspoon garlic powder

Makes 4 cups

Melt the butter in a saucepan over medium heat. Stir in the onion and cook until tender. Add in remaining ingredients and bring to a boil. Reduce heat to low and simmer 30 minutes.

Originally printed in the News-Leader, August 2006

Tahini Sauce

1/3 cup sesame seed paste
1/2 cup water, or more as needed
1 - 2 tablespoons fresh lemon juice
1 1/2 teaspoons garlic, minced
1/2 teaspoon salt
Pinch of cayenne

Makes about 1 cup

In a blender, combine all the ingredients. Process on high speed to make a creamy sauce. Adjust seasoning to taste. Great served with falafels (see page 16).

Originally printed in the News-Leader, April 2005

Ozarks Moms are talking about

Desserts & Sweets

Almond Chocolate Fruitcake Loaf

2 cups almonds, sliced
1 stick butter
7 ounces almond paste
1/2 cup brown sugar
2 teaspoons vanilla extract
1 tablespoon orange zest, grated
3 eggs
1/2 cup flour
1/2 teaspoon baking powder
1 cup semi-sweet chocolate chips
2 cups dried cherries, chopped
1/2 cup white raisins, chopped

Serves 8

Preheat oven to 325 degrees.
Grease a 4-1/2 x 12-1/2-inch loaf pan and line completely with wax paper; grease the paper. In a large bowl, beat together butter, almond paste and sugar with an electric mixer until well blended. Beat in vanilla and zest. Add eggs, one at a time, beating well. Add in flour and baking powder. Stir in chocolate chips, cherries, raisins and almonds until well mixed. Scrape batter into loaf pan.

Bake about 1 hour, or until cake springs back when touched lightly and top is golden. Let cake cool in pan 40 minutes, and then unmold cake by lifting with wax paper onto a wire rack and let cool completely. Carefully peel off wax paper. Wrap cake in plastic wrap and then in aluminum foil. Refrigerate at least 2 weeks before serving or up to 3 months, brushing every few days with the liquor of your choice. I would suggest amaretto or maybe Godiva chocolate liqueur.

Originally printed in the News-Leader, November 2006

A Simple Chocolate Glaze

3 squares (3 ounces) unsweetened
   chocolate, chopped
5 tablespoons unsalted butter,
   cut into pieces
Pinch salt
1 3/4 cups sifted powdered sugar
4 to 5 tablespoons hot water
1 teaspoon vanilla

Makes about 1-1/2 cups

Use a small heatproof bowl set over simmering water on low heat (water should not touch bottom of bowl). Combine in the bowl chopped chocolate, butter and salt. Stir often until smooth. Remove from heat and hot water.

Add powdered sugar and 2 tablespoons hot water and whisk well to combine. Gradually add the remaining hot water to achieve a thick glaze consistency. Whisk in vanilla. Let stand at room temperature 5 minutes, whisking occasionally, to thicken slightly.

Slowly pour glaze onto top center of the cake (or whatever you are glazing). Working quickly, tilt the cake to allow the glaze to cover the cake and then run down the edges. You must work quickly as the more time you take the quicker the glaze sets and the harder a shell you will have. When glaze is set, wrap the glazed food loosely and store in refrigerator. Let stand at room temperature 15 to 20 minutes before serving.

Originally printed in the News-Leader, October 2006

Baklava

2 pounds filo dough
 (approximately 40 sheets)
4 cups walnuts, finely chopped
4 cups pistachios, finely chopped
1 1/2 cups sugar
1 1/2 tablespoons cinnamon
1/2 teaspoon ground clove
3/4 pound unsalted butter
 (melted)

Honey Syrup for Baklava:
2 cups honey
1 1/2 cups water
1 tablespoon fresh lemon juice
1 teaspoon ground clove
1 teaspoon ground cinnamon
Zest of one lemon
Zest of one orange
Pinch of salt

Serves 12

Butter a 13×9-inch pan on the bottom & sides and set aside.

In a food processor, process the pistachios, walnuts, sugar and cinnamon until ground and set aside.

Cut the filo sheets into 13×9-inch sheets. They need to fit snug in the pan.

Lay 8 sheets of the cut filo dough into the greased pan brushing a little butter between each sheet.

Sprinkle 2 cups of the walnut/pistachio mixture into the pan. Lay 6 more sheets of filo on top. Apply more melted butter between each sheet. Repeat this 3 more times so that you have 4 separate layers of the pistachio/walnut mixture.

Finish the top with the remaining sheets, butter it as well.

Using a very sharp, serrated knife, carefully score the baklava into diamond shapes. Try to cut about half-way down into the baklava when you do this.

Bake for 50 to 60 minutes at 325 degrees until nice and brown.

Remove the baklava from the oven and very carefully drain the excess butter.

Set the baklava on a cooling rack, and pour the honey syrup mixture through a strainer to completely over it.

Cover the baklava and let sit for at least 4 hours or overnight.

To serve, cut through the score marks with a sharp knife.

Honey Syrup:
Combine all of the ingredients in a saucepan and bring to a simmer for at least an hour. When done simmering set the syrup aside to cool.

Originally printed in the News-Leader, September 2005

Banana Bread Pudding

4 1/2 cups stale French bread
   cubed into 3/4-inch pieces
1 cup bananas, sliced 1/4-inch
   thick
3 eggs
1/2 cup banana, pureed or
   mashed
1/4 cup white sugar
1/2 cup brown sugar
2 cups milk
2 teaspoons vanilla extract
1/2 teaspoon salt
1/2 teaspoon nutmeg
1 teaspoon cinnamon
1/2 cup pecans, lightly toasted
4 tablespoons butter

Serves 6

In a bowl beat the eggs with the milk, pureed banana, vanilla, cinnamon, sugar, nutmeg and salt. Pour the mixture over the bread cubes in a bowl. Allow to sit for half an hour under refrigeration. (Feel free to add in another beaten egg and half cup of milk if the pudding looks dry.) The cubes need to be soaked through.

Remove from refrigerator and add in the pecans and the sliced bananas and pour into a buttered 2-quart casserole dish. Dot the top with butter and bake uncovered at 375 degrees for 40 minutes or until knife inserted in the center comes out clean.

Serve hot with crème Anglaise or a little slightly whipped heavy cream with some maple syrup added to it. For a little more elegance, bake the bread pudding in individual ramekins so each diner gets their own.

Originally printed in the News-Leader, March 2004

Basic Shortcake

3 cups flour
3 tablespoons sugar
1 1/2 tablespoons baking powder
3/4 teaspoons salt
12 tablespoons cold, unsalted
   butter, cut into small pieces
1 1/2 cups heavy cream
2 teaspoons vanilla extract

Serves 4-6

Sift the flour, sugar, baking powder and salt into a large bowl. Toss with a fork to combine. Cut the butter into the flour mixture with a pastry cutter or a fork until the largest pieces of butter are the size of peas.

Combine the cream and vanilla in a liquid measure. Make a well in the center of the flour and pour the cream mixture into the well. Mix with a fork until the dough is evenly moistened and just combined; it should look crumbly and still feel a little dry. Gently knead by hand five or six times to create a loose ball.

Turn the dough out onto a lightly floured work surface and pat it into an 8-inch square, 3/4- to 1-inch thick. Transfer the dough to a baking sheet lined with wax paper and cover with plastic, then chill for 20 minutes in the refrigerator. Heat the oven to 425 degrees.

Originally printed in the News-Leader, August 2006

Berry Cobbler in Cast Iron

3 tablespoons cornstarch
1/4 cup cold water
1 1/2 cups sugar
1 tablespoon lemon juice
4 cups frozen berries of your
   choice
1 cup flour
1 teaspoon baking powder
1/2 teaspoon salt
6 tablespoons butter, cold, cut in
   small pieces
1/4 cup boiling water

Serves 6

In a large bowl, stir together the cornstarch and 1/4 cup cold water until cornstarch is completely dissolved. Add 1 cup sugar, lemon juice and berries; combine gently and pour into a 9-inch cast iron skillet.

In a bowl, combine the flour, remaining sugar, baking powder and salt. Blend in the butter until the mixture resembles coarse meal. Add 1/4 cup boiling water and stir the mixture just until a soft dough is formed.

Bring the berry mixture to a boil, stirring. Drop spoonfuls of the dough carefully onto the boiling mixture, and bake the cobbler on a baking sheet the middle of a preheated 400-degree oven for 20 to 25 minutes or until the topping is golden.

Blackberry Upside-Down Cake

1/4 cup brown sugar
2 tablespoons butter
3 cups blackberries
1/2 cup butter
1 3/4 cups sugar, divided
2 eggs
1 1/2 cups flour
2 teaspoons baking powder
1/2 teaspoon salt
1 teaspoon vanilla

Serves 4

Preheat oven to 350 degrees.
Heat the brown sugar and 2 tablespoons butter in a 9-inch iron skillet over medium heat. Add in the berries and cook, stirring until bubbly.

Add 3/4 cup of the sugar to the pan and crush the berries slightly.

Cook for about 5 minutes, and then remove from heat and set aside.

Cream 1/2 cup butter and remaining sugar until light. Blend in the eggs. Mix flour, baking powder and salt together and add alternately with milk to the creamed butter/sugar mixture. Stir in the vanilla.

Pour batter over cooked fruit in pan and bake for 35 minutes. When the pan has cooled slightly, run knife around edge of pan and turn onto a cutting board.

Garnish with whipped cream.

Originally printed in the News-Leader, June 2005

Cantaloupe Pops

6-ounce can frozen lemonade
    concentrate
4 cups cubed cantaloupe or other
    melon
3/4 cup water
10 paper drink cups (small)
Ten wooden popsicle sticks

Makes 10 servings

In blender or food processor, combine lemonade concentrate and cantaloupe and process until smooth.

Fill each drink cup with about 1/3 cup of this mixture, then freeze until partially frozen, about 1 hour.

Insert wooden sticks and freeze until firm. To serve, peel away the paper cup. About 10 pops

Originally printed in the News-Leader, July 2006

Caramelized Mango-Lime Tapioca

4 cups milk
3/4 cup white sugar
1/2 cup quick-cooking tapioca
2 large eggs
1 1/2 teaspoons finely grated
    lime peel
1/4 teaspoon salt
2 teaspoons vanilla extract
2 ripe mangos, peeled, pitted and
    diced
16 teaspoons brown sugar

Makes 8 servings

Combine the milk, sugar, tapioca, eggs, lime peel and salt in a medium sized saucepan. Stir together well and then let sit for about 5 minutes. Place the pan over medium high heat until the tapioca comes to a boil. Be sure to stir constantly as this happens. This will take around 10 minutes. Be careful not to burn or scorch the pudding at this point.

When thick, pour the pudding into a large shallow bowl and mix in the vanilla. Place in the refrigerator and allow to cool. When cool, cover the top with plastic wrap

When ready to eat, preheat your oven broiler to high.

Place some of the diced mango into each of eight cups or ramekins that measure about 1 cup each. Spoon some of the pudding onto the mango and smooth over the top. Leave some room at the top as well.

Sprinkle 2 teaspoons brown sugar over each of the puddings.

Place the puddings on a sheet tray together. Place underneath the broiler and broil until the sugar bubbles all over. Serve warm.

Originally printed in the News-Leader, May 2006

Cherry Clafouti

Vegetable cooking spray
1/2 cup sour cherries, pitted
2 tablespoons sugar
2/3 cup nonfat buttermilk
4 tablespoons sugar
3 tablespoons flour
2 teaspoons brandy
1 egg, lightly beaten
1 teaspoon powdered sugar

Serves 2

Coat two 5-ounce ramekins or custard cups with cooking spray. Place 1/4 cup cherries into each ramekin and sprinkle with sugar; set aside.

Combine buttermilk and next four ingredients, stirring with a wire whisk until well blended. Pour evenly over cherries.

Place ramekins on a baking sheet. Bake at 375 degrees for 35 minutes or until puffed and set. Sprinkle the top of each with powdered sugar.

Chocolate Eggnog

4 eggs separated
1/2 cup brown sugar
2/3 cup unsweetened cocoa
   powder
1 tablespoon vanilla extract
1 1/2 cups milk
4 ounces rum
1/8 teaspoon salt
1 1/2 cups heavy whipping cream
1/3 cup semi-sweet chocolate,
   grated

Serves 4

In large bowl, beat together yolks, sugar, cocoa and vanilla until thick and smooth.

Slowly stir in milk and rum. Beat whites with salt to soft peaks.

Fold whipped cream into chocolate mixture, gently fold in whites.

Chill and serve.

Originally printed in the News-Leader, December 2006

Chocolate Pecan Pie

6 ounces unsalted butter
5 ounces semi-sweet chocolate
    (bar form)
3 large eggs
1/2 cup sugar
1 1/2 cups light corn syrup
1 tablespoon bourbon
    (optional or to taste)
1 1/2 cups chopped pecans
1 (10-inch) pie shell, par-baked

Serves 8

In a small sauce pan over low heat melt the butter. Add chocolate and stir until melted. In a medium bowl, combine eggs, sugar and corn syrup. Slowly stir in chocolate mixture. Stir until thoroughly combined.

Stir in the bourbon. Place chopped pecans in the par-baked 10-inch pie shell. Pour chocolate mixture over nuts to fill the shell. Gently stir to combine.

Bake at 325 degrees until filling sets, approximately 20 to 30 minutes.

Originally printed in the News-Leader, November 2004

Chocolate Scones with Macerated Cherries

Macerated Dried Cherries:
1 cup dried sweet cherries
2 tablespoons rum
2 tablespoons water

Scone Dough:
2 cups all-purpose flour
1/2 cup confectioners' sugar
2 1/2 teaspoons baking powder
1/8 teaspoon cream of tartar
1/2 teaspoon salt
6 tablespoons butter, cut into
    small pieces
1/2 cup heavy cream
2 large eggs, at room temperature
1 1/2 teaspoons vanilla extract
1 1/2 ounces dark chocolate,
    chopped

Makes 12 servings

Macerated Dried Cherries:
Place cherries, water and rum in bowl. Stir and let stand uncovered for 2 hours.

Scone Dough:
Preheat oven to 400 degrees.
Line a baking sheet with parchment paper. Whisk together flour, sugar, baking powder, cream of tartar and salt in mixing bowl. Cut in butter until small, pearl-size bits form using pastry blender.

Whisk together heavy cream, eggs and vanilla extract in another small bowl. Add egg mixture to dry ingredients.

Drain the cherries and add to the mixture with the chocolate. Stir just until mixed. Dough will be slightly sticky to touch.

Turn dough onto floured work surface and knead briefly 6 to 8 times. Pat dough into 9-inch round disc. Cut into 12 wedges. Place on baking sheet, about 2 inches apart. Bake for 18 minutes or until golden brown. Serve warm as is or cool

Crème Brulee with Tropical Fruit

2 cups whipping cream
1/2 cup sugar
1 tablespoon candied ginger,
   ground
1 vanilla bean, split lengthwise
   and scraped or 1 tablespoon
   vanilla extract
5 large egg yolks
12 teaspoons sugar
Sliced tropical fruit (such as
   mango, banana and kiwi)

Makes 6 servings

Preheat oven to 325 degrees.

Place 6 3/4-cup ramekins or small coffee cups in a roasting pan. Mix cream, sugar and ginger in heavy saucepan. Scrape the seeds from vanilla bean. Add seeds and bean to saucepan. Stir over medium heat until sugar dissolves and mixture comes to simmer. Cover pan, reduce heat to low and simmer 10 minutes, then strain.

Whisk yolks in medium bowl until well blended. Gradually whisk in hot cream mixture just to blend. Divide among dishes. Pour enough hot water into pans to come halfway up sides of dishes.

Carefully transfer pan to oven. Bake custards until almost set in center when pans are gently shaken, about 30 minutes. Using a spatula, transfer custards dishes to work surface; cool 30 minutes.

Chill at least 3 hours and up to 2 days. When ready to eat, turn your oven broiler on and move the rack up to the highest level. Sprinkle 2 teaspoons sugar evenly over each custard. Place custard cups under the broiler for about 1 minute or until sugar dissolves and browns.

Refrigerate until custards are firm again but topping is still brittle, at least 2 hours. Garnish crème brulees with tropical fruit.

Originally printed in the News-Leader, February 2006

Éclairs

2 cups milk
1 cup milk
8 ounces sugar
1/4 teaspoon salt
8 egg yolks
4 ounces cornstarch
3 ounces butter
2 tablespoons vanilla extract

Makes 36 puffs or 18 éclairs

In a medium sized pot, bring 2 cups milk and half the sugar to just boiling.

In a medium bowl, whisk together 1 cup of milk with the cornstarch until well dissolved. Add the yolks, salt and remaining sugar and whisk together thoroughly. Add a small amount of the hot milk to the cold milk/egg mixture and stir well.

Whisking constantly, add the warmed milk and egg mixture to the pot with the hot milk. Cook over medium high heat stirring constantly until it comes to a boil. Remove from the stove and strain into a clean bowl.

Place over an ice water bath, stirring slowly until the pastry cream cools slightly, then stir in chunks of butter and vanilla extract. Continue to stir until cold.

Cover with plastic wrap and refrigerate.

Éclair Pastry:
1 1/4 cups water
3/4 cup unsalted butter, cut into
  pieces
1/2 teaspoon salt
1 1/2 cups flour
4-6 large eggs

Chocolate Ganache:
8 ounces semi-sweet chocolate
  morsels
1 cup heavy cream

Éclair Pastry:

In a heavy saucepan bring water to a boil with butter and salt over high heat. Reduce heat to moderate and add the flour all at once and beat with a wooden spoon until mixture pulls away from sides of pan, forming a dough.

Transfer dough to bowl of a standing electric mixer and beat in 4 eggs, one at a time, on high speed, beating well after each addition. Batter should be stiff enough to just hold soft peaks and fall softly from a spoon. If batter is too stiff, in a small bowl beat remaining 2 eggs lightly, one at a time, and add to batter a little at a time, beating on high speed, until batter is desired consistency.

Preheat oven to 425 degrees and line baking sheets with parchment paper.

Pipe about 36 mounds onto baking sheets, each about 2 inches in diameter and leaving 1-1/2-inches between mounds. With a finger dipped in water gently smooth pointed tip of each mound to round puffs.

Bake puffs in upper third of oven 10 minutes, switching position of sheets in oven halfway through baking if necessary. Reduce temperature to 400 degrees. Bake puffs 20 minutes more, or until puffed and golden. Let stand in turned-off oven 30 minutes.

Transfer puffs to racks to cool. With a skewer poke a 1/4-inch hole in the lower side of each puff.

Chocolate Ganache:

Heat cream to boiling. Pour over the chocolate. Stir until melted

To Assemble:

Use a pastry bag to pipe the cream filling into each puff through the hole that was made earlier. Make sure to pipe filling into the top of the puff as well as the bottom.

Take a spatula and frost the top of the puff with the chocolate.

Originally printed in the News-Leader, September 2006

Frosting "Perfectly Chocolate"

1 stick (1/2 cup) butter
2/3 cup Hershey's Cocoa
  (see if you can find the Dutch
  process version)
3 cups powdered sugar
1/3 cup milk
1 teaspoon vanilla extract
1 teaspoon almond extract

Makes approximately 2 cups

Melt the butter and stir the cocoa in well. Mix in the powdered sugar. Slowly add in the milk, beating until smooth. You can add some extra milk if needed to thin out the frosting if desired. Stir in vanilla and almond.

Originally printed in the News-Leader, July 2006

German Friendship Cake

Starter:
1/4 cup flour
1/2 cup water
1/8 package dry yeast

First Day and Fifth Day:
1/4 cup flour
1/4 cup milk
1/4 cup white sugar

Tenth Day:
2 eggs
2/3 cup vegetable oil
2 cups flour
1 cup sugar
1 1/2 teaspoons baking soda
2 teaspoons baking powder
1/2 teaspoon salt
2 teaspoons cinnamon
2 teaspoons vanilla
1 (20-ounce) can crushed
  pineapple, drained
1/2 cup dried cranberries
1/2 cup chopped pecans

Topping:
1/4 cup butter
1 cup brown sugar
1 tablespoon flour

Makes 1 cake

Mix the starter ingredients in a bowl and let stand covered at room temperature for 24 to 36 hours.

Place the starter in a medium bowl and combine it with the "First Day" ingredients. Stir once a day for 5 days.

Cover and refrigerate.

On the fifth day, place in a larger bowl and add the" Fifth Day" ingredients which duplicate the first day. Stir once a day for 5 more days.

Cover and refrigerate.

Combine all of the" Tenth Day" ingredients with the remaining starter.

Pour into a greased and floured 9x13-inch pan. Combine topping ingredients and sprinkle on top.

Bake at 350 degrees for 40 to 50 minutes.

Originally printed in the News-Leader, March 2007

German's Sweet Chocolate Cake

1 package German's sweet chocolate
1/2 cup boiling water
1 cup butter
2 cups sugar
4 egg yolks, unbeaten
1 teaspoon vanilla
1/2 teaspoon salt
1 teaspoon baking soda
2 1/2 cups flour, sifted, minus
    5 tablespoons
1 cup buttermilk
4 egg whites, stiffly beaten

Coconut-Pecan Frosting:
1 cup evaporated milk
1 cup sugar
3 egg yolks
1/4 pound butter
1 teaspoon vanilla
1 1/3 cups Baker's Angel Flake
Coconut
1 cup chopped pecans

Makes 2-2/3 cups

Melt chocolate in boiling water; cool.

Cream butter and sugar until fluffy. Add egg yolks one at a time and beat well after each. Add melted chocolate and vanilla. Mix well.

Sift together salt, soda and flour. Add alternately with buttermilk to chocolate mixture, beating well. Beat until smooth. Fold in beaten egg whites.

Pour into three 8- or 9-inch cake layer pans, lined on bottoms with paper. Bake in a 350-degree oven 30 to 40 minutes. Allow to cool. Frost tops only.

Frosting:
Combine first five ingredients. Cook and stir over medium heat until thickened (about 12 minutes). Add 1-1/3 cups Baker's Angel Flake Coconut and 1 cup chopped pecans. Beat until thick enough to spread.

Originally printed in the News-Leader, November 2003

Gratin of Fruit with Biscotti Topping

1 1/2 pounds Granny Smith apples
1 1/2 pounds firm ripe pears
3 tablespoons lemon juice
1 tablespoons lemon rind, grated
1/2 cup sugar
1/4 cup dried currants or white
    raisins
2 tablespoons rum (optional)
5 to 6 ounces almond biscotti or
    ginger snap cookies
1 tablespoon melted butter
1 teaspoon ground cinnamon
1/3 cup half-and-half
2/3 cup pear nectar
Cool Whip if desired

Serves 6

Peel and core apples and pears. Cut fruit lengthwise into about 1/2-inch thick wedges; place in a large bowl. Add rind and juice to apples and pears, along with sugar, currants, and rum; mix gently. Pour into a shallow 2 to 2-1/2-quart baking dish.

Place biscotti in a 1-quart zip-lock plastic bag and crush lightly with a rolling pin to make 1-1/2 cups coarse crumbs; pour into a small bowl. Add butter and cinnamon and mix. Sprinkle crumb mixture evenly over fruit. Pour cream evenly over topping.

Bake in a 375 degrees oven until fruit is tender when pierced with a fork and crumb topping is browned, 30 to 40 minutes. Let gratin cool at least 10 minutes; serve warm or cool. Scoop onto plates or bowls and top with Cool Whip.

Green Tomato Pie

8 very green tomatoes
2 tablespoons lemon juice
1 teaspoon grated lemon peel
1/2 teaspoon salt
1 teaspoon cinnamon
3/4 cup granulated sugar
2 tablespoons cornstarch
1 tablespoon butter
Pie dough for a 2-crust, 9-inch pie

Serves 8

Cut a small x on the bottom of each tomato. Dip the tomatoes in the boiling water for about 60 seconds, then into the ice water. Peel and slice the tomatoes.

In a saucepan, combine tomatoes with lemon juice, lemon peel, salt and cinnamon and cook the mixture over low heat, stirring frequently.

Mix together the sugar, cornstarch and two tablespoons of water and stir into tomato mixture.

Cook the tomatoes until they look clear, stirring constantly. Add in the butter, remove from heat and let stand until slightly cooled.

Pour the tomato filling into the bottom pie crust. Cover with top pastry, seal edges, crimp, and cut some small slits in crust to allow steam to escape.

Bake at 435 degrees for 35 to 45 minutes or until nicely browned. Serve warm or cooled.

Holiday Cranberry Pie

3 cups cranberries, washed
1 cup golden raisins
1 cup light brown sugar
1/2 cup water
3 tablespoons all-purpose flour
1/4 cup orange juice
1 teaspoon grated orange peel
1 teaspoon vanilla extract
2 tablespoons butter
Pastry for double-crust, 9-inch pie

Serves 8

Preheat oven to 450 degrees.
In a large, heavy saucepan, combine all ingredients except vanilla and butter and bring to a boil. Lower heat to medium-low and, stirring frequently, gently boil the mixture for 10 to 15 minutes until it thickens. Remove from heat and stir in the vanilla.

Pour filling into an unbaked, pastry-lined, 9-inch pie shell and dot with butter. Cover the pie with the other pastry. Cut a few vent holes into the pastry top and crimp edges.

Bake at 450 degrees for 10 minutes. Reduce heat to 350 degrees and bake 35 minutes more or until golden brown.

Originally printed in the News-Leader, November 2005

Holiday Eggnog Cheesecake

1 cup graham cracker crumbs
1/4 cup sugar
1/4 teaspoon ground nutmeg
1/4 cup melted butter
1/4 teaspoon cinnamon
3 (8-ounce) packages cream
  cheese, softened
1/2 cup sugar
1/2 cup brown sugar
3 tablespoons cornstarch
3 eggs
2 egg yolks
2 cups eggnog
1 teaspoon vanilla
1/2 teaspoon freshly grated
  nutmeg

Serves 12

Combine crumbs, sugar, nutmeg, cinnamon and melted butter; press into bottom of 9-inch spring form pan.

Mix the cream cheese, sugars and cornstarch on high speed in a mixer until completely blended. Add in the eggs one at a time, scraping the bowl after each addition.

Blend in the eggnog, vanilla and nutmeg.

Pour into the spring form pan and bake at 350 degrees for 15 minutes. Open the oven to let out the heat, then reduce the heat to 250 degrees and bake for an additional hour or until the cake is firm in the middle.

Open the oven door and allow to cool naturally for an hour.

Allow to sit refrigerated overnight before cutting.

Originally printed in the News-Leader, September 2006

Honey Pumpkin Pecan Pie

3 large eggs
1/3 cup honey
1 (16-ounce) pumpkin
1/2 teaspoon salt
1 teaspoon cinnamon
1/4 teaspoon ground cloves
1/2 teaspoon ground ginger
2 cups pecan halves

Topping:
3 large eggs
1/2 cup light brown sugar
3/4 cup honey
2 tablespoons butter, melted
2 1/2 teaspoons flour
1/4 teaspoon salt

Makes 2 pies

In a large bowl, whisk together first seven ingredients. Divide and pour into 2 prepared pie shells.

Arrange pecans on top of each pie. Set aside until topping is ready.

Preheat oven to 350 degrees. Set a large baking sheet in oven to preheat.

Topping:
In a large bowl, whisk together eggs, brown sugar, honey, butter, flour and salt until well mixed. Pour over pecans.

Bake both pies on preheated baking sheets for 45 minutes, or until filling in center is set.

Remove from oven and cool on rack before serving.

Originally printed in the News-Leader, November 2004

Key Lime Meringue Pie

3 egg yolks
1 1/4 cups sugar
1/4 teaspoon salt
1/3 cup cornstarch
3 cups water
3 tablespoons butter
1/3 cup Key lime juice
3 tablespoons grated fresh lime
   peel
4 egg whites, at room temperature
Pinch of salt
4 tablespoons sugar
1/4 teaspoon cream of tartar
1 pre-baked 9-inch pie shell

Makes 8 servings

Beat the egg yolks until they start to turn yellow, then set aside. Combine sugar, salt and cornstarch in a medium sauce pan and slowly add in the water stirring well with a whisk.

Bring to a boil, stirring constantly, and boil for about two minutes.
Remove the pan from the heat.

Temper the eggs by whisking in a small amount of the starch mixture into the reserved egg yolks.

Add in a little more starch and whisk again well. Finally add in the rest of the cooked starch

Add in the butter and lime juice and stir well.

Return the saucepan to stove and boil 2 minutes.

Remove from the heat and add in the lime peel. Pour into pie shell.

Combine the egg whites, cream of tartar and salt in a medium bowl and beat until foamy. Add in 1/4 cup sugar and continue to beat till the sugar dissolves and meringue is stiff.

Cover pie filling with meringue. Bake at 350 degrees until very lightly browned.

Originally printed in the News-Leader, July 2006

Lemon Chess Pie

2 cups sugar
1/4 cup margarine, melted
1 tablespoon flour
1/4 cup milk
1 tablespoon cornmeal
1/4 cup lemon juice
4 eggs, unbeaten
Pinch salt
Pie shell, unbaked

Serves 8

Combine all ingredients and stir just enough to mix.

Pour into unbaked pie shell and bake at 375 degrees for about 35 minutes or until filling is set.

Orange Chiffon Cake

8 ounces cake flour, sifted
1 1/2 cups granulated sugar
1 tablespoon baking powder
1 teaspoon salt
4 ounces vegetable oil
6 egg yolks
2 ounces water
4 ounces orange juice
1 tablespoon orange zest
1 tablespoon vanilla extract
8 ounces egg whites

Glaze:
3 ounces powdered sugar, sifted
2 tablespoons orange juice
2 teaspoons orange zest

Serves 10

Sift together the flour, 3/4 cup of sugar and the baking powder and salt. In a separate bowl mix the oil, yolks, water, juice, zest and vanilla. Add the liquid mixture to the dry ingredients.

In a clean bowl, beat the egg whites until foamy. Slowly beat in the remaining 3/4 cup of sugar. Continue beating until the egg whites are stiff but not dry. Stir one-third of the egg whites into the batter to lighten it.

Fold in the remaining egg whites. Pour the batter into an ungreased 10-inch tube pan. Bake at 325 degrees until toothpick comes out clean, approximately 1 hour.

Immediately invert the pan over a parchment covered sheet pan. Let the cake sit upside down until completely cool. Then remove from the pan.

Stir the glaze ingredients together in a small bowl and drizzle over the top of the cooled cake.

Originally printed in the News-Leader, May 2005

Orange Honey Cheesecake

1 cup graham cracker crumbs
1/4 cup walnuts, finely chopped
2 tablespoons butter or margarine,
   melted
1/2 teaspoon ground cinnamon
2 tablespoons sugar
4 (8-ounce) packages cream
   cheese, softened
1 cup honey, divided
3 tablespoons cornstarch
1 teaspoon vanilla
4 eggs
1 1/2 tablespoons orange peel,
   grated

Serves 12

Preheat oven to 325 degrees. Mix together cracker crumbs, walnuts, butter, cinnamon and the 2 tablespoons sugar. Press firmly into the bottom of a 9-inch spring form pan.

Beat the cream cheese, 1/2 cup of the honey, the cornstarch and vanilla in large bowl with electric mixer on medium speed until well blended. Add eggs, one at a time, mixing on low speed after each addition just until blended. Stir in orange peel; pour over crust.

Bake for 20 minutes, then turn oven heat down to 250 degrees and bake for another hour or until center is almost set. Run knife or metal spatula around rim of pan to loosen cake; cool before removing rim of pan. Refrigerate overnight. Drizzle with remaining 1/4 cup honey just before serving.

Originally printed in the News-Leader, June 2005

Pavlova

4 egg whites
1 pinch salt
1 cup of sugar
1 tablespoon cornstarch
1 teaspoon lemon juice
1 teaspoon vanilla extract
Whipped cream
Peaches, berries or any other soft
   fruit that is in season for
   garnish

Serves 4

Preheat the oven to 200 degrees. Beat the egg whites into a foam. Add the salt and beat until soft peaks form that fold over when the beater is removed.

Slowly beat in the sugar, beating well after each addition. Keep beating until the mixture is stiff and the peaks stand up. Mix in the cornstarch, lemon juice and vanilla extract.

Line an oven tray with wax paper. Spread the meringue into a circle using a piping bag with a star tip. Bake in an oven for 2 to 2-1/2 hours. Turn off the heat and leave in the oven overnight to cool. Top with whipped cream and fruit just before serving.

Originally printed in the News-Leader, August 2006

Peach Granita

1 1/2 pounds peaches
3 tablespoons lemon juice
1 cup sugar
3/4 cup water
1/2 cup peach preserves
1/2 cup peach schnapps

Makes 8 servings

Blanch the peaches in boiling water, then place them in cold water to help remove the skins. Remove the peach pits and puree the peaches in a food processor. Add the lemon juice to the peach puree to prevent browning. Combine the water and sugar over low heat and stir until the sugar is dissolved. Add the preserves to the sugar water to melt. Combine the peach-flavored sugar water, peach puree and peach schnapps and pour into a chilled pan, then set in the freezer.

Let the granita freeze for about two hours or until slushy. After two hours stir the mixture every 20 minutes as it sets and freezes. Continue this for around 2 hours. This breaks up the ice crystals as they form and will give you an icy texture. To serve, scrape an ice cream scoop across the ice and form a ball. Serve in a martini glass with a few fresh raspberries and a splash of a sweet white sparkling wine.

Originally printed in the News-Leader, September 2003

Peach Ice Cream (as it was meant to be)

1 quart heavy whipping cream
1 quart whole milk
1 vanilla bean, with the seeds
   scraped out and reserved
2 tablespoons vanilla extract
2 cups sugar
2 tablespoons almond extract
4 cups fresh, tree-ripened peach
   puree with a few small chunks
   remaining
Pinch of salt

Serves 10

Only to be made with the ripest, juiciest and sweetest peaches money can buy

Combine the milk and cream with the sugar, vanilla bean and vanilla bean seeds in a heavy bottomed saucepan. Bring this mix to a simmer, stirring to dissolve the sugar, then reduce the heat and allow the vanilla bean to steep to infuse flavor for 20 minutes. Pull out the vanilla bean but do not strain out the vanilla seeds.

Add in the remaining ingredients and cool in the freezer until very cold but not frozen. Process in an ice cream maker per the maker's instructions.

Remember, the longer it takes to freeze ice cream the smoother the texture will be.

Originally printed in the News-Leader, September 2005

Peach Pie Cobbler

Crust:
4 cups all-purpose flour
2 sticks butter, chilled, cut into
  small pieces
1 cup shortening, chilled
1/2 teaspoon salt
7 tablespoons ice water

Filling:
10 cups peeled, pitted and sliced
  fresh peaches
3 tablespoons fresh lemon juice
1 cup sugar
2 teaspoons almond extract
1 teaspoon ground cinnamon
1/4 teaspoon fresh-grated nutmeg
1/4 cup all-purpose flour

Serves 8

Prepare the crust: place flour, butter, shortening and salt in a large bowl. Using a pastry blender or two knives, cut the butter and shortening into the flour until the mixture looks like peas. Roll out the dough to roughly the size of a 9x13-inch pan.

Combine all of the filling ingredients and place in a buttered 9x13-inch pan.

Cover with the crust tucking it in at the sides. Cut a vent hole in the top, then bake at 350 degrees until the top is golden brown and the fruit is bubbly.

Originally printed in the News-Leader, June 2005

Pecan Date Pie

1 (9-inch) pie crust, unbaked
3/4 cup butter
3/4 cup brown sugar
2 egg yolks
1/2 cup evaporated milk
2 egg whites
1 cup pecans, chopped
1 cup dates, chopped
1/8 teaspoon powdered cloves
1/4 teaspoon cinnamon

Serves 8

Cream the butter, add sugar and beat until creamy. Add the egg yolks one at a time. Blend in the milk, spices, pecans and dates. Beat the egg whites until stiff and fold into mixture.

Pour the mixture into pie crust and spread evenly. Bake 40 minutes at 350 degrees.

Serve with whipped cream.

Originally printed in the News-Leader, November 2004

Pfefferneusse

1/2 cup shortening
3/4 cup packed brown sugar
1/2 cup molasses
3 drops anise oil or ground star
  anise
1 egg
1/2 teaspoon baking soda
1 tablespoon hot water
3 1/2 cups all-purpose flour
1/4 teaspoon salt
1/2 teaspoon ground cinnamon
1 teaspoon ground ginger
1/8 teaspoon white pepper

Makes 2 dozen cookies

Preheat the oven to 350 degrees.
In a medium bowl, cream together the shortening and brown sugar until smooth. Mix in molasses, anise oil and egg. Dissolve baking soda in hot water and stir into the mixture.

Combine the flour, salt, cinnamon, ginger and white pepper; blend into the molasses mixture until uniform.

Knead for a minute until easy to work with. Shape dough into 1-inch balls, and place 1 inch apart on ungreased cookie sheets.

Bake for 10 to 12 minutes in the preheated oven until slightly browned on the bottom.

Originally printed in the News-Leader, May 2005

Pineapple Rhubarb Pie

1 cup water
2 cups frozen rhubarb
1 cup sugar
3 tablespoons cornstarch
2 tablespoons water
1 large can crushed pineapple,
  drained
1 teaspoon lemon zest

Serves 8

Combine the water, sugar and rhubarb in a medium saucepan and bring to a simmer. Cook until the rhubarb is tender.

Add in the pineapple and zest and stir well.

Combine the extra water and cornstarch and add to the fruit. Bring the fruit mixture up to a boil and boil for about 2 minutes then allow to cool slightly.

Pour into a graham cracker crust and allow to set up in the refrigerator overnight.

Serve with whipped cream.

Pumpkin Cheesecake with Walnut Crust
& Ginger Cranberry Sauce & Chantilly Cream

24 ounces cream cheese
1/2 cup sugar
1/2 cup brown sugar
3 tablespoons cornstarch
4 eggs
1/2 cup heavy whipping cream
2 cups canned pumpkin
1 tablespoon vanilla extract
1 tablespoon cinnamon
2 teaspoons nutmeg
1 teaspoon ginger

Serves 12

Pumpkin Cheesecake:
In the mixing bowl combine the cream cheese, sugars and cornstarch. Whip on high speed until well combined.

Add in the eggs one at a time, turning the speed of the mixer down to medium. TIP: crack the eggs on a flat surface, then open into a bowl or saucer and add the egg to the cheese mixture. This will help prevent shells from getting into the cake.

Turn off the mixer and scrape the bottom of the bowl after each egg addition. Turn the mixer to low and add in the whipping cream, pumpkin, vanilla and spices. Scrape the bowl.

Pour the cheesecake batter into the prepared spring form pan. TIP: the batter should come about three-fourths of the way up the side of the pan. Do not overfill. The cake will rise during the baking process and you do not want it to overflow. Smooth the cheesecake batter out by tapping the pan on the counter or with a spatula.

Place the cheesecake into a preheated 350-degree oven. TIP: set a time for 15 minutes. After the initial 15-minute baking time open the oven door and let the heat out for 20 to 30 seconds.

Turn the oven heat down to 250 degrees and close the door. Continue to bake for another 45 to 60 minutes. When the cake is done you can tap on the side of the pan and the cake will move as a whole. TIP: it is very important to not over bake the cake as this is one of the major causes of cracking.

Remove the finished cake from the oven and run a knife around the inside of the pan. This will separate the cake form the sides. Let the cake sit for about 30 minutes. Unlatch the spring form pan and remove it. Place the cake in a refrigerator and let rest overnight.

Walnut Crust:
2/3 cup butter, melted
2 cups graham wafer crumbs
3/4 cup walnuts
1/4 cup sugar
1/4 teaspoon cinnamon
1/4 teaspoon nutmeg

Ginger Cranberry Sauce:
1 tablespoon walnut oil
1 tablespoon ginger, minced
2 cups dried cranberries
Zest and juice of 3 oranges
2 tablespoons brown sugar
1/2 cup water

Chantilly Cream:
1 cup heavy whipping cream
2 tablespoons brown sugar
2 teaspoons vanilla extract

Walnut Crust:
Using a food processor or knife chop the walnuts and sugar together until they are fine. TIP: processing the nuts and the sugar together will keep the chopped nuts from getting gummy. Combine the nuts with all of the remaining crust ingredients and mix well.

Press firmly into the bottom of a 10-inch spring form pan. I personally do not like to put crumbs on the sides of cheesecakes. I think they can make the cake uneven at the top.

Ginger Cranberry Sauce:
In a non-reactive saucepan, sauté the ginger and the zest in a small amount of walnut oil until soft, about 3 minutes.

Add the cranberries, juice and sugar. Simmer for 30 minutes until very soft. Cool the sauce, then process in a food processor or blender using a little extra water to reach the desired consistency.

Chantilly Cream:
Place the mixing bowl, whisk or attachments into the freezer for half an hour before attempting to whip the cream. This will help the cream whip faster. Keep the whipping cream in the refrigerator until ready to whip.

Put all the ingredients together in a large stainless steel bowl. Whisk the cream just until it holds its shape. Refrigerate the cream until ready to use.

Originally printed in the News-Leader, October 2005

Quick Chocolate Rice Pudding

2 cups cooked white rice
1 1/2 cups milk
1/3 cup white sugar
2 teaspoons vanilla extract
1/3 cup pecans
1 tablespoon butter
3 tablespoons unsweetened cocoa

Serves 4

In the top of a double boiler over simmering water, combine all ingredients except for the rice. Cook until smooth.

Mix in the cooked rice and simmer until heated throughout.

Originally printed in the News-Leader, March 2006

Quickie Yogurt Parfait

1 pint vanilla yogurt
3 tablespoons honey
1/2 cup Grape-Nuts
1/2 cup fresh blueberries
1/2 cup fresh strawberries
A few extra berries for garnish

Serves 2

Blend yogurt, honey and fruit. Add on additional berries and top with Grape-Nuts.

7UP Cake

1 1/2 cups butter,
   room temperature
3 cups sugar
5 eggs
3 cups flour
2 tablespoons lemon extract
1 teaspoon lime zest
1 teaspoon lemon zest
3/4 cup 7UP
1/4 cup confectioners sugar

Makes 1 cake or about 16 servings

Cream the butter and sugar until smooth.
Add eggs, one at a time, beating well after each and scraping down the sides of the bowl.

Add in the flour, lemon extract, both zests and the 7UP; mix well.

Pour into greased angel food pan. Bake at 325 degrees for 1 hour and 15 minutes or until done.

Sprinkle with powdered sugar.

Originally printed in the News-Leader, May 2006

Scottish Shortbread

1 pound flour
3 ounces sugar
1 ounce candied lemon peel
  (see page 155)
1 ounce almonds,
  blanched and chopped
1/2 pound room-temperature
  butter
4 ounces melted butter

Makes 12 servings

Rub the room-temperature butter into the flour with a pastry blender. Stir in the melted butter and the remaining ingredients and mix lightly

Roll out the mixture onto a floured board. Use your hand or a rolling pin to roll the dough into a round shape about an inch and a half thick

Pleat the dough with your fingers around the edges. Use a fork to make a few decorative lines across the top. Finally, use a knife to mark out about 12 triangles. This is where the cookies will be cut after baking. Place a few pieces of the candied peel on top.

Bake at 300 degrees on a tray for around half an hour or until the shortbread is light brown. Allow to cool on a wire tray.

Originally printed in the News-Leader, February 2006

Sugar Cream Pie

1 1/3 cups granulated sugar
1/2 cup flour
1 pint heavy cream
1 teaspoon vanilla
1 unbaked 9-inch pie shell
2 teaspoons ground nutmeg
3 tablespoons butter

Serves 8

Mix sugar with flour in a mixing bowl. Add in cream and vanilla and stir well.

Pour into pie shell and dot with butter. Bake in preheated 500-degree oven for 5 to 7 minutes. Stir ingredients in shell and bake 5 minutes longer. Stir again, then reduce oven temperature to 350 degrees.

Bake about 30 minutes longer or until knife inserted in center comes out clean. Cool before cutting.

I actually like mine served right out of the fridge. The texture is much better this way.

Originally printed in the News-Leader, April 2004

Tiramisu

1 1/2 cups espresso
1/2 cup sugar
1/2 cup Tuaca or any liqueur of
   choice

Filling:
4 egg yolks
1 1/2 cups sugar
2 cups cream cheese
1 teaspoon vanilla extract
2 teaspoons fresh orange zest
36 Ladyfinger cookies
4 ounces semi-sweet chocolate,
   grated

Serves 8

Combine the espresso, liquor and sugar mix well and set aside.

Over a double boiler, beat egg yolks and 1/2 cup sugar with a whisk until mixture lightens in color and forms ribbons. Allow to cool 5 minutes.

Beat cream cheese with 1 cup sugar. Add in the vanilla extract and the orange zest.

Fold softened cream cheese into egg yolk mixture one quarter at a time.

Line a loaf pan with enough plastic wrap that the sides of the wrap hang over either side.

Dip the Ladyfinger cookies in the coffee-sugar-liquor mixture and lay them along the edges of mold, lining the entire mold bottom as well as the sides. Fill the mold one-third full with the cheese and egg mixture and sprinkle with chocolate.

Dip more Ladyfingers into the coffee mixture and lay across the top of the cheese mixture. Add on more of the cheese and egg, topping with shaved chocolate. Place another layer of the soaked Ladyfingers on top.

Wrap the tiramisu with the leftover plastic wrap and gently push down on the top to help the ingredients settle. Allow to sit overnight to firm up.

When ready to serve, turn the mold over, remove the tiramisu from the pan and cut into wedges.

Originally printed in the News-Leader, November 2006

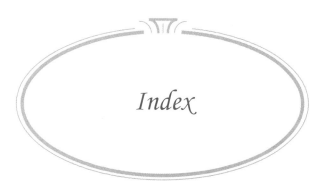

Index